SAFARI PRESS

Ask the Whitetail Guides

Ask the Whitetail Guides

by

J. Y. Jones

Safari Press Inc.

Jones, J. Y.

First edition

Safari Press Inc.

2007, Long Beach, California

ISBN 1-57157-237-6

Library of Congress Catalog Card Number: 2005931714

10 9 8 7 6 5 4 3 2 1

Printed in China

Readers wishing to receive the Safari Press catalog, featuring many fine books on big-game hunting, wingshooting, and sporting firearms, should write to Safari Press Inc., P.O. Box 3095, Long Beach, CA 90803, USA. Tel: (714) 894-9080, or visit our Web site at www.safaripress.com.

This book is dedicated to whitetail enthusiasts everywhere, and specifically to those who are committed to hunting whitetails ethically and with good conservation of the species as a top goal. Furthermore, I dedicate the book to those organizations, made up almost exclusively of hunter-conservationists, who are an important part of the engine that drives whitetail management all across the great continent of North America. Many of these organizations consist of small local hunting clubs that do their part by educating their members in good management techniques, involving themselves in habitat improvement, and contributing data (jawbones, kill statistics, and the like) to a state agency for compilation. Some are larger statewide bodies, and a few are national and international in scope. In addition, I dedicate the book to the large number of hunter-conservationists who are devoted members of the various state game agencies involved in whitetail management. Every state except California, Alaska, and Hawaii has a huntable whitetail population, and it is no small task to apply judicious governmental oversight.

No animal is loved so deeply, pursued with as much vigor, or defended with as much fervor as the white-tailed deer. To all who contribute to this amazing endeavor, I offer them a tip of my camouflage cap, and they may consider themselves a part of those to whom this book is dedicated.

Finally, as I intend with all my books, I dedicate this effort to the eternal God, the Great *I Am*, the self-existent and uncaused Creator of Heaven and Earth and all contained therein. May He judge me one day and find me worthy, not because of anything I have done, but because of the grace He has extended to me in allowing me to know Him intimately through His son, Jesus Christ. All glory to the Father, the Son, and the Holy Spirit!

Table of Contents

Foreword

If you intend to travel to another state to take a trophy whitetail, you need a guide. The best deer hunter in Texas, if picked up and set down in Alberta (or Pennsylvania or Montana or Michigan or Kansas) would be totally lost for a week or two, perhaps for a whole season. This would be just as true of an experienced hunter from any of those whitetail hot spots transported to Texas or any of the others.

The white-tailed deer is so adaptable that he can make his home—and make himself scarce—almost anywhere: in deserts or swamps, high mountains, prairies, or forestlands. I have hunted whitetails in all these habitats and more, from the tropics to Canada and from sea to shining sea, which is why I know that, no matter how gifted a deer hunter you may be, you will usually be wasting your time trying to take a mature buck when you are away from your own familiar hunting grounds.

That's why you need a guide. He usually has access to prime country. He will know the local terrain, deer habits, timing of the rut, preferred forage plants, weather changes, and the reactions of the game to hunting pressure, etc., all of which are likely to be quite different from your own stomping grounds. He may even know already where a candidate buck hangs out. You're certainly free to go out into strange terrain and rely on blind luck to find a trophy animal, but I regret to inform you that a trophy buck on his own ground is very likely to be "luckier" than you are.

I've hunted with a lot of whitetail guides. Most of them were good guys as well as ethical hunters, but some were better than others, especially in terms of understanding the needs and wishes of hunters who may have saved up for years to make an out-of-state hunt for the buck of a lifetime.

A careful study of this book will help you understand the variables in choosing a guide for an important hunt. Better yet, it will offer new perspectives on how to hold up your end of the deal once the hunt begins. That adds up to a more memorable experience . . . and a more successful hunt.

John Wootters
(Editor emeritus of *Petersen's Hunting* and author of thousands of deer hunting articles)
Ingram, Texas
August 14, 2005

Introduction and Acknowledgments

This book comes about as a direct result of the success of its predecessor in this series, *Ask the Elk Guides*. Before that book was even off the presses, it had sold more advance copies than all my previous books combined. Safari Press, and specifically publisher Ludo Wurfbain, had correctly surmised that there existed among hunters a hunger for hunting information directly from the best source, namely the people who actually guide hunters for the animal. As sales of the first book did increasingly well, I was commissioned to do a second. Because of the huge numbers of hunters of white-tailed deer in North America and the corresponding wider range of hunting conditions and situations, I decided to expand the number of guides interviewed to eighteen, including three for each of the chapters on different kinds of whitetail hunting. As with *Ask the Elk Guides*, there are five chapters covering specific questions on various aspects of whitetail hunting, then six chapters on different locations and situations for hunting whitetails, and a final catchall chapter to wrap it up.

Many of the questions are exactly the same as in the elk book, but a few that are more specific to whitetail hunting have been added, and some have been modified to apply more explicitly to whitetail hunting. The white-tailed deer is a much different animal from its elk cousin, so the guide responses are sufficiently dissimilar that readers will certainly enjoy the information, even if they've already read *Ask the Elk Guides*.

Naturally, I find myself indebted to many people in compiling this volume. In 2004 I sent out a call to all my contacts in the hunting and outdoor-writing fraternity, asking for guidance in finding eighteen of the best possible whitetail guides. I relied heavily on information provided by these people, and I think we've done it. Perhaps we missed a few top guides who should have been included, as is likely always the case, but I did try diligently to separate the good from the very best.

People who supplied one or more names include well-known hunter and writer Craig Boddington; Scott Rupp, editor of *Petersen's Hunting*; Duncan Dobie, editor of *North America Whitetail*; Pat Bollman and Mike Rogers Sr., both former presidents of Safari Club International; Brent Sinclair, considered by many to be the best overall guide in North America; Ryk Visscher, president of the Alberta Professional Outfitters Association; Dennis Campbell, president of the Grand Slam Club; Don Causey, publisher of *The Hunting Report*; Stan Moody, a personal friend and himself a Maine guide, and also a state legislator there; Kirk Kelso, who suggested his brother Keaton; and fellow hunters Jim Dodd, Olivia Angelloz, Doug Lugar, Mike Borel, and Ward Jones.

I offer a special thanks to Bill Honza, a professional photographer in Ennis, Texas, who allowed me to use many of his images throughout the book. I want to especially thank the guides who have submitted to the required intensive interviews, and who have provided most of the pictures found in this book. Many thanks again to publisher Ludo Wurfbain for assigning me this project. I would also like to thank Linda, my wife of forty-one years, for permitting me the time away to conduct and type up the interviews and then to assemble them into book form.

My apologies if I missed anyone who contributed. I hope that the effort has been worth it, and that the reader will be blessed with a wealth of new information from reading this volume.

Note to readers: J. Y. Jones can be reached at www.jyjones.com.

Author's best Coues buck.

Chapter 1
MEET THE WHITETAIL GUIDES

It is with great pleasure that I introduce whitetail hunters everywhere to perhaps the best assemblage of whitetail guides ever featured in one piece of literature.* From the youngest to the oldest, these guides are the most experienced group imaginable, and each has guided for an average of more than twenty-five years. Most are still actively outfitting and guiding, though a couple of them have ceased taking paying hunters and now hunt only for themselves. Whichever the case, all have a wealth of information to share, and what they have to say may open your eyes to a whole new world with respect to guide-client relations. I believe that anyone who has ever been guided on a whitetail hunt will find himself described somewhere in the pages of this book.

These guides share a large number of characteristics in common. They universally place a high premium on hunter ethics, honesty, integrity, hard work, patience, dependability, and persistence. They all desire their hunters to come well prepared in every possible way, and they go into great detail delineating how one goes about doing this. Despite the commonality of such thoughts, their individual words are unique and different, so the reader never gets bored.

These guides are truly excellent representatives of the outdoor fraternity, and I think you'll agree they all offer invaluable insights into the world of whitetail hunting. I can't think of a sufficient way to repay them for imparting their wealth of experience to us, the whitetail hunters of today, so thank them yourself when you see them . . . and enjoy these guys to the utmost!

**Each guide can be found here in the sequence they appear in the book, with a brief summary of their backgrounds and experience, contact information, and a recent photograph. The material included here is taken directly from interviews with the guides, and in some cases from printed material they supplied. Most information in this book has been obtained by means of telephone interviews with each guide, and is essentially as they said it.*

Hal Blood
Cedar Ridge Outfitters
36 Attean Road, P.O. Box 744
Jackman, ME 04945
207-773-3003

Hal began guiding about 1990, and he got into it because it was kind of a dream of his to do full-time what he loved best. He originally was a lobsterman on the coast of Maine, and ever since he was a kid he had a powerful love of hunting and fishing. He decided to make it his way of life, and that's what he did. He still actively guides in the big woods of northern Maine, and he says he has no idea how many hunters he has personally guided. All his guided hunts are one-on-one, and he estimates that he's guided perhaps a hundred or more clients personally over the years. He has guided many times that figure for black bear, so his overall guiding experience encompasses several hundred hunters.

Hal guides mostly because of the sheer enjoyment of it, but also it's now become his primary livelihood. He doesn't read as much in hunting magazines and other periodicals as he used to, but the "big three"—*Sports Afield, Outdoor Life,* and *Field and Stream*—have always been his favorites. He's strongly turned off by the trend toward more and more advertising in the outdoors and hunting articles he reads. His own book, "Hunting Big Woods Bucks," is a classic work on hunting Maine's deer.

Jeff Charles
P.O. Box 245
Strong, ME 04983
207-684-3035
antlerhill@adelphia.net

In 1985 Jeff and his wife purchased a small sporting camp on the shores of Sebec Lake in Maine. It had been their lifelong dream to have such a place, and they decided to go for it. Jeff had already been doing some guiding, but not in any organized fashion. He's now been professionally guiding for some twenty years, and he still actively guides his clients. He has guided approximately two hundred fifty hunters personally over the years, ranging from eight to twenty a season. He guides because of a love for the big woods, and it's a pleasure to him just to be out there, especially when he has an affable hunter with whom to share the time. He considers the woods his office, because he literally spends the whole year in them. He reads *Deer Hunter* magazine, and also *Field and Stream*, as far as national publications go. He also enjoys a number of local magazines, notably the *North Woods Journal* and the *Maine Sportsman*.

Dan Rosman
The Sanctuary
13450 Buchanan Road
Stanwood, MI 49346
231-972-7722
rosman@tucker-usa.com

Dan moved to northern British Columbia as a kid and ended up living with a family that had a hunting outfit. He was an integral part of that family for ten years. They taught him about guiding when he was fifteen years old, and he's been guiding ever since. By now, he has approximately twenty-six years of overall guiding experience. Until 1988, he guided for Stone sheep, moose, caribou, and other animals in British Columbia. He's still an active guide. Since 1988, he has been guiding pretty much only for whitetails, mainly in Michigan but a little in eastern Oregon and eastern Washington.

One big reason he guides is the pleasure of being outdoors, but he's quick to state that the biggest reason is that he enjoys the satisfaction of making a hunter happy. He has personally guided about three hundred hunters altogether, and he's always interested in seeing their reactions in field situations. An avid reader, he takes in every hunting magazine he can get his hands on, including *Petersen's Hunting, North American Hunter, Safari,* and "almost all the main ones." As far as hunting books go, he isn't particular; he reads any appealing one that comes along.

Chris Pevey
Millhaven Plantation
1705 Millhaven Road
Sylvania, GA 30467
800-421-8043
912-531-7823
www.millhaven.com

Chris got his wildlife technician degree from Abraham Baldwin Agricultural College in Tifton, Georgia, and first came to Millhaven Plantation as an intern as part of his curriculum. He began by trapping nuisance beavers for Millhaven, and as he learned the terrain he began guiding hunter-clients for turkey, soon adding deer hunts to his job description. He had planned to go on to the University of Georgia for further studies, but changed his mind when he was offered a full-time job at Millhaven .

Chris went from assistant game manager to head game manager, and under his leadership the program has continued to grow. He manages 54,000 acres in Georgia and South Carolina, a sizable tract of land anywhere but almost beyond precedent in today's Southeast. He still guides actively, and he's personally guided many hundreds of hunters, although he hasn't kept records of this figure and can't say exactly how many.

He loves sharing the outdoor experience with other people, saying that there's nothing like helping people experience success while out hunting. He's a huge supporter of quality deer management, so for reading material the *QDM Journal* is his favorite magazine of all time. He also enjoys *Gray's Sporting Journal*, which is owned by his employer, William Morris. Chris says that it's his dreaming journal because he often dreams of someday being able to do some of the hunts featured in the magazine. He also enjoys reading *Wildlife Trends*.

Charles Ruth
South Carolina Department of Natural Resources
P.O. Box 167
Columbia, SC 29202
803-734-8738
ruth@dnr.sc.gov

Charles got involved in guiding while he was in graduate school working on a master's degree in wildlife biology. Rather than just standing around when he wasn't doing something associated with his schoolwork, he took the initiative to help with guiding on the Cedar Knoll Club in Allendale, South Carolina. The club was owned by Hayward Simmons who took Charles under his wing and showed him the ropes. Charles worked with Simmons for six or seven years and picked up a wealth of information on whitetails and how to hunt them.

After finishing school, Charles moved to the lower Coastal Plain of South Carolina for the research, management, and guiding opportunities there. He feels this is a fantastic area for deer hunting because of the rich, dense habitat that is among the best in the country. He does not currently guide professionally, although he does sometimes guide in a noncommercial manner. He's guided at least six hundred hunters in his career.

He likes to hunt, a characteristic he feels is a prerequisite for guiding. He also likes animals, and naturally he has a particular interest in deer. He reads very few of the popular media magazines because he puts little stock in them. Charles is an avid archer, so he does take *Bowhunting* magazine, mainly to keep up with the changes in bowhunting gear. He continues to be involved in research, so he is more inclined to read scientific literature because he has more confidence in that kind of material.

Jay Steen
Westervelt Lodge
P.O. Box 89
Demopolis, AL 36732
800-281-7991
205-373-8212
www.westervelt.com

Jay started guiding in 1981 at Westervelt Lodge, and he's been guiding there ever since. He points out that, in Alabama and most places in the Southeast, it's called guiding, but guides are not actually on the stand with the clients most of the time. Since he started, he's guided many hundreds of hunters. To him, guiding provides a living, but it's also enjoyable for him to meet people from every profession and every walk of life. As Jay says, it sure beats having to get up and go to a real job! Mainly, to him it's just an enjoyable way of life. He reads *Buckmasters*, and also *North American Whitetail*. Additionally, there are several local Alabama publications that he enjoys, and he's always on the lookout for articles about hunting in various newspapers.

David Davis
Maverick Outfitters
3926 Crestridge Street
Brownwood, TX 76801
325-643-4182
ddhunt@web-access.net

David started guiding about 1981. He worked on the Nail Ranch in Albany, Texas, for some years, and then came back down to central Texas to continue his guiding career. When David returned to central Texas, he was induced to come down and work at some places in the southern part of the state. So David has guided all over Texas—north, central, and south. He still actively guides, and he estimates he has had between six hundred and eight hundred personal clients.

He guides because he loves white-tailed deer, and guiding gets him into the woods with them more. He doesn't read most of the hunting magazines anymore because they've become so "commercialized." He still enjoys reading the works of people such as Craig Boddington, who for the most part isn't out to sell anything with his articles, and that's a hard thing to find now, according to David. As far as books go, he reads wildlife management books more than any other kind. One of the guys he works for has coauthored a book that embodies twenty years of management experience, and he views that book as a kind of Old Testament of deer management. He points out that now guys are starting to write the New Testament, but in most cases he thinks they're "reinventing the wheel and selling it."

Mike Gardner
San Miguel Hunting Ranches
7010 Highway 71 West, #340
P.O. Box 303
Austin, TX 78735
512-288-5848
www.sanmiguelhunts.com

Mike started guiding full-time on his father's ranch in central Texas while he was still in high school, some twenty years ago. After that, he guided part-time for a south Texas outfitter, and then in 1997 he started the company that he now owns. He is not just an owner, but also still an active guide. He has personally guided three hundred to four hundred hunters for deer, and perhaps two hundred for turkeys. Some of his hunts are 2x1 guided, so on those hunts he guides two hunters. He guides about 50 percent of the clients personally. He guides purely because he enjoys it. He points out that it is a business, too. Sometimes he thinks he'd make more money if he spent more time in the office, but he really prefers to be in the field.

Mike says that if you're going to guide for a living, you have to do it because you enjoy it and you like interacting with the customers. He likes to meet all kinds of interesting people from around the country and from all walks of life. That, combined with the sheer enjoyment and love of being out in the field and the outdoors, makes it hard for him to stay in the office during hunting season. Mike and his wife have a son coming soon, and he expects that to change his life radically.

He enjoys reading material by Larry Weishuhn, who is one of the pioneers of Texas whitetail hunting, along with John Wooters, Murphey Ray, and Al Brothers. He reads *Texas Trophy Hunter* magazine and *North American Whitetail*, as well as Cabela's *Outfitter's Journal*. He also likes reading African works by authors such as Peter Capstick.

Don White
Rancho San Enrique
401 Breckenridge
Boerne, TX 78006
830-249-8519
dlwhite@gvtc.com

Don started guiding in the mid-1990s, and he did it to help pay for his deer lease in Mexico. Subsequently he went from a lease arrangement with the Mexican landowner to strictly package hunts. The decision to do this was made by the owner, but Don was asked to stay on and run the guiding operation. He still actively guides, and has personally guided more than a hundred hunters for deer in Mexico. He likes the challenge of finding a good deer and getting a hunter close enough to get a good shot at the animal. It's been a kind of evolution of hunting for him, as with many guides. To him, the most enjoyable part of the hunt is trying to figure out a deer so that it can be taken. He loves guiding because the challenge is there to get a deer not just for himself, but for other people, too.

Don subscribes to his favorite magazine, *North American Whitetail.* He's always been fascinated with the work of Mike Biggs, a Texas writer and photographer, who has several books and videos out, such as *Whitetails in Action.* Don credits Mike with being simply a great photographer. What is especially interesting about Mike's work is that he will sometimes take several pictures of the same deer over a two- to five-year period, which allows one to see vividly how the deer ages and matures.

Eric Albus
Milk River Outfitters
P.O. Box 35
Hinsdale, MT 59241
406-648-5494
www.milkriveroutfitters.com
ealbus@nemontel.net

Eric started guiding for a friend in 1989, mainly for mule deer. His family owned some good property on the Milk River; they formed an association with some of their neighbors and began managing for better quality whitetails on that piece of land. They enjoyed great success at it, and around 1995 Bill Jordan of RealTree came to hunt with them, raising their national profile considerably. The rest is history.

Eric was born and raised in the area where he guides, and has guided some two hundred fifty hunters personally for whitetails over the last fifteen years or so. He actively guides hunters every fall. He has no pat answer for why he guides, but high on his list is the enjoyment he gets from seeing the outdoor experience through the eyes of another individual who lives in a world of concrete and steel, a thought that gives him a deeper appreciation for what he does for a living and the wonderful place where he lives. He sees in this a renewed perspective for how grateful he should be for all the blessings he has had in life, to be able to live the lifestyle he loves.

Eric has been married to his wife, Robyn, for more than twenty years, and they have two sons, Cole and Kyle. Eric frankly says that he does very little reading in hunting magazines and other hunting literature.

Keaton Kelso
K&K Outfitters
1723 James Court
Newton, KS 67114
316-772-0854
www.duckandbuck.com
keaton@duckandbuck.com

Keaton has been hunting ever since he got old enough to stand upright beside his father. Guiding runs in the family, and Keaton and his brothers have been in the whitetail business for about eighteen years. About six years ago Keaton and one of his brothers opened K&K Outfitters. The operation began in Kansas, but they've branched out into Missouri and, more recently, into Nebraska as well.

Keaton actively guides during the season, and he's out in the woods every day, doing most of the management of their properties. He's personally guided over 150 people for whitetails, but when turkey and waterfowl hunters are counted his total guiding experience goes up to the 500 to 600 range. He subscribes to the three stages of being a hunter: the killing stage, the trophy-hunting stage, and, finally, the enjoyment-of-the-hunt stage. Keaton firmly believes he's at that third stage already, even though he's still fairly young. He hunted over 100 days last season, although he was hunting for himself only two or three days during that time.

He gets just as much excitement, and even more fun, out of his client shooting a big buck as he does when he pulls the trigger himself. His favorite magazine is *Petersen's Hunting*. He also likes almost any bowhunting publication because he gets so much good information out of them that the rifle-oriented magazines don't cover.

James Woodley
Heartland Outfitters
480 South Meadowbrook Rd.
Springfield, IL 62707
217-773-3003
www.heartlandoutfitters.com
mjmw2@adams.net

James started guiding for whitetails in 1998. He first got a master's degree, and in the process an internship was a required part of the curriculum. He hooked up with Heartland Outfitters and landowner Dr. Bob Russell, and when his internship was completed there was the offer of a job. The doctor needed some help, so James decided to stay and work for him. His original degree was in parks and recreation management, but he subsequently obtained a specialty degree in wildlife management as well. He's thus unusually educated in both the business part and the management part of the guiding business. Despite this, he still actively guides deer hunters each season, and has personally guided about one hundred twenty hunters.

James guides because it's part of his vocation, but also because he simply likes hunting and really gets himself involved in it. He also likes helping people realize their goals, and seeing satisfaction in them from the hunting experience. As far as reading habits go, *Bowhunter* magazine is one of his favorites. He also reads *Deer and Deer Hunting* and *Petersen's Bowhunter*. Bowhunting is mainly what is done on the properties he manages, so naturally he gravitates toward those specialty kinds of publications.

Gary Drinkall
P.O. Box 2215
Chetwynd, BC,
Canada V0C 1J0
250-788-2115
gmdrink@telus.net

Guiding comes naturally in the Drinkall family. Gary's father, Glen Drinkall, ran a Stone sheep/moose/grizzly operation out of Toad River, British Columbia, for several decades, and his other son, Dale, is still involved there. Gary was twelve years old when he started out horse wrangling, and he was eighteen when he started actually guiding in Canada's Northwest Territories. That same year he started guiding for whitetails in Alberta. He's been guiding now for about eighteen years, and he still guides every year. He's taken some fifteen hunters personally every year, so he figures he's guided about two hundred fifty to three hundred hunters for all species.

Gary guides because he really gets a charge out of getting somebody into position to kill a good deer, and economics has little to do with his satisfaction. He also likes the country where he hunts. He points out that you can only shoot so many deer for yourself, so guiding prolongs his enjoyment of the hunting season. It really thrills Gary to figure the buck out for the hunter, and then let the hunter do the rest.

He reads everything he can get his hands on about whitetails, because "you can never figure them out completely, so you need all the help you can get." He remarks that he really likes reading stories such as those in *Big Buck* magazine. Another of his favorites is *Eastman's Journal*. Gary tends to avoid the regular hunting magazines because he doesn't believe they're credible much of the time.

Rene and Kelly Semple
South Paw Outfitters Ltd.
P.O. Box 505, Sangudo, AB,
Canada TOE 2A0
780-785-3404
www.southpawoutfitters.com

Rene (pronounced "Renny") and Kelly are the only husband-and-wife team included in this book. The Semples started outfitting in 1991 when they began guiding for black bear; they quickly expanded to include moose, elk, and white-tailed deer. Today, they make their living from their white-tailed deer operation.

The Semples take pride in offering a first-class hunting experience, and a testament to their quality of service is the high number of return clients. For Rene and Kelly, having repeat hunters return to deer camp year after year is like welcoming old friends or family back home. From Rene's perspective, a quality guide is someone who gets as much enjoyment from the hunt as his client does. It may be said that the work of a quality guide takes place behind the scenes rather than in what you see.

Rene has a wide range of interests, and when he's not guiding or preparing for hunters, he is snowmobiling, flying, or working on some activity outdoors. In his quest for knowledge, Rene has become well-read on a wide range of subjects. Kelly's activities include being executive director of the Hunting for Tomorrow Foundation in Alberta and acting as first vice president for the Alberta Professional Outfitters Association.

When asked about hunting and how it relates to their day-to-day lives, the couple jokingly replies, "Doesn't everyone's life revolve around hunting 24/7?"

We should all be so lucky.

Jim Shockey
185-911 Yates Street, Suite 340
Victoria, BC, Canada V8V 4Y9
888-826-1011
www.jimshockey.com

Jim started guiding professionally about fifteen years ago. He went to a well-known outfitter who had, in Jim's opinion, the best black bear territory in the world, and offered to guide for him. The outfitter must have needed no help, because he turned Jim down. Since he wanted to guide so badly, Jim offered to guide free of charge. That proposition seemed attractive to the outfitter, so he let Jim do it. He loved it so much that he guided for free for two years, and though he doesn't do it for free anymore, he still actively guides. He has guided over three hundred hunters personally. He guides because he loves it, pure and simple, and he strongly feels that it's the best lifestyle a person could ever have.

Jim's reading interests run far beyond hunting literature; he's fascinated with history, art, adventure, exploration, and such. Historical exploits have a strong relationship to adventure hunting, according to Jim, and that's part of their appeal for him. As far as hunting periodicals go, he reads most of them but prefers *American Hunter, North American Hunter, Petersen's Hunting,* and some regional Canadian publications that he considers excellent. He also likes the specialty whitetail magazines, such as *Big Buck*.

Jim not only guides, but he's also an avid black-powder hunter. Having taken all the North American big-game animals (all of them record-book quality specimens) using a muzzleloader, he's begun to hunt in Africa and elsewhere. He's now a television personality and has achieved such celebrity status that he's recognized in the hunting community wherever he goes. He is an avid writer with several books and hundreds of articles to his credit.

Duwane Adams
Arizona Big Game Hunts
204 Avenue B
San Miguel, AZ 85631
520-385-4995
www.arizonabiggamehunting.com

Craig Boddington got Duwane into guiding. Duwane took Craig on a Coues deer hunt, and afterwards Craig told him, "You need to get a guide license, because you're that good!" Duwane replied, "You've got to be kidding me. How would I get any clients?" He said, "I'll send them to you." And that's how Duwane got his guiding business started back in 1979. He notes that both he and Craig have come a long way since then. Duwane feels a deep debt of gratitude to Craig because he got him started and he's been a great friend to him. As Duwane says, "God bless him for it."

Duwane still loves to guide hunters, and he does so at every opportunity. At the time of this interview, he had personally guided hunters successfully to 170 Coues bucks, of which 23 made the B&C book. To Duwane, guiding is like a drug, and he thanks God that it's legal. After becoming an accomplished Coues deer hunter on his own, he started guiding by taking all his friends hunting. The bottom line is that he just couldn't get enough of Coues deer hunting, and he notes that this is still true.

As far as reading preferences go, Duwane firmly believes that you can't read enough, especially about Coues deer hunting, because of a dearth of material on the subject. He gives seminars all over the United States, and he has written an incisive book, *How to Hunt Coues Deer*, that provides great insight on hunting this subspecies. He'd like to see more Coues deer articles in the general hunting literature, because it's one of the most challenging species to hunt in North America.

Carlos Gonzalez Hermosillo
Avenida Sauzales #44
Col. Guanjas Coapa
Mexico, DF 14330, Mexico
52-555-671-2064
huntmexico@huntmexico.com

Carlos began guiding in Sonora about thirty years ago, and he actually began his career seeking large Coues deer for his clients. He is very involved in running his guiding business these days, but every year he still actively guides clients personally. He has personally guided about three hundred deer hunters, about 30 percent of them for desert mule deer and the remainder for Coues deer. He has also guided quite a few hunters for desert bighorn sheep. He guides for the same reason as most other guides, namely because he likes to hunt, and guiding has been important to his personal satisfaction in life.

Carlos loves to help people achieve their goals in hunting while immersing himself in something he likes doing. He says he enjoys guiding someone to a trophy deer as much as he enjoys taking one himself. He adds that he reads everything that has "hunting" written on it, and he loves all hunting books, magazines, and videos. He asserts, however, that the videos lately are becoming too commercially oriented and that they often leave out the real facts about hunting.

Kirk Kelso
Pusch Ridge Outfitters
11077 East Escalante Road
Tucson, AZ 85730
520-544-0954
www.puschridgeoutfitters.com

Kirk started guiding hunters about 1986. He guided one year for another outfitter but then decided to go into business for himself. When people heard that he was taking some great bucks, they started contacting him. Not long after going into business for himself, he moved most of his operation to Sonora, Mexico. Most of his guiding occurs there now because he can't generate enough volume to make a living off Coues deer hunting in his home state. Arizona has a rigid draw system, and even if he puts in fifteen to twenty guys, perhaps only five of them draw successfully. In Sonora, he's able to take up to one hundred hunters per year, and nobody has to draw a tag, making it a much more dependable source of income.

Kirk manages his camps personally, but he also gets out and does plenty of hands-on guiding during every camp rotation. He finds satisfaction in being able to take people hunting, helping them kill a nice buck, and seeing the pleasure they get out of the experience. He notes that there's nothing quite like it.

When it comes to reading habits, he enjoys the SCI publications, particularly *Safari* magazine, noting that many of his hunters belong to SCI. He takes his outfit to the SCI convention every year and finds a lot of enthusiasm for the kind of hunting he offers. He also likes to read *The Hunting Report* because he believes it keeps you up to date on what's going on around the world with regard to hunting. Kirk is also a fan of the Grand Slam Club publication *Grand Slam/Ovis*.

Chapter 2

SELECTING AN OUTFITTER/ GUIDE FOR WHITETAILS

What should a hunter look for in an outfitter/guide?

Hal Blood: He should look for quality accommodations, food, equipment, and so on. He should also check references. I get people calling all the time, and they always ask the same questions. Even before they say hello, they are asking about our success rate and how much our hunts cost. These are not the first questions they should ask, but maybe the last ones. There's a lot of stuff they need to know first, like I mentioned above, such as what kind of food they should expect, what services are included, and whether there are any hidden charges they need to know about.

A lot of people in the same field are charging quite a broad spectrum of prices, so the hunter needs to know what that price includes. Experience is important, too, but I know there are a lot of good young people out there who are guiding hunters, and they may do a good job, but they don't have the experience of guiding people yet. A good way to break in is to work for someone else for a while, and maybe meet a lot of people and learn the ropes. I didn't do that, though. I went straight from catching lobsters to guiding for deer, and it's tough. I had to find some people who were willing to say, "You've never taken anybody hunting before, but that's OK; I'll give you a chance."

Jeff Charles: To me, it seems you need to look for someone who's knowledgeable but who also really takes care of the client. The guide needs to be able to assess the client's abilities, to administer first aid, and to protect the client's safety. The deer is actually secondary when compared to the best interests of the client/hunter. A lot of the guides with whom I've worked think only of the deer, and they forget about

Whether the weapon is a rifle or bow, the guide's preparation makes all the difference to the hunter. (Photo courtesy of James Woodley)

the client. You know, we've got guys coming up here who sit at a desk all year, and they're with us for only five days. I look at them and say, "This guy's not going to be able to hunt the way we'd like him to, so we've got to cater to him." I'd recommend an outfitter and guide who is going to look out for your interests, no matter what kind of shape you're in.

Dan Rosman: The first thing to look for is honesty and a good reputation, and also someone who's been around for a while. There are a lot of fly-by-night outfitters who put on a good show and talk a good line, but they just don't get it done.

Chris Pevey: Results are a big thing that comes to mind. I know that when I'm looking for a guide for a hunt of my own, I don't want to see pictures of what they killed ten years ago. I want to see what they did last year and the year before. Success ratios are important, and so is the way they treat their hunters. You have to look at the overall situation.

Charles Ruth: First and foremost, look for someone who has a good reputation, who's known for integrity, and who's willing to give you references. Look for a person who will spend some time initially with you on the phone, and will discuss and shoot straight with you about successes as well as failures. They need to tell you the best times to come on a hunt, and be honest about it. Understand that I was dealing with a 140-day season when I was guiding, and the best times varied tremendously within that four-and-a-half-month interval. You ought to be able to weed out a lot of potential outfitters and guides from a simple phone conversation.

Jay Steen: The hunter shopping for a hunt should look for a reputation that's solid. He should be able to talk to past clients and find out what kind of experience they had. It also depends on what type of hunt he's wanting. If he wants a Texas-type hunt, he doesn't need to talk to people in Texas and then come to Alabama expecting that type of hunting experience. If he wants to hunt like we hunt in Alabama, then we've got that kind of experience, but it's different from Texas and most other places.

David Davis: First, the hunter needs to find a guide who hunts good country. If you're going to kill a good whitetail, you've got to be starting less than sixty miles from one. Whitetails are probably more like that in this respect than most other species. For example, within a sixty-mile circle around my house, the only direction you could go to kill a big whitetail would be west. So pick an outfitter who's in the right country. Pick an outfitter who's truthful and who doesn't promise you the moon. I believe you can usually tell, because some of these guys sound like used-car salesmen.

Everybody has a picture of a big deer to show you, so you can't go by that. When I call an outfitter and ask how many deer he killed last year, he might say he killed so many and that the biggest one scored 160. What I want to see is a picture of the biggest and a picture of the smallest deer he killed last year. If only one guy killed a 160, and the next ten guys behind him killed a 110, then that tells you something. References are good, but they can be deceptive because everybody's got cousins, nephews, and so on who will tell you anything they want you to hear. I'd want to talk to a guy who killed a nice deer and also to someone who didn't kill a deer at all, and see what kind of experience each had.

Mike Gardner: You really need look at what your goals are, and where you are in your hunting career, and have honest expectations. Clients should realize that they're going on a *hunt*. Since it is a hunt, they should make it a point to enjoy all aspects of the experience, and not just focus on harvesting an animal. As regards honest expectations, if the best deer you've ever taken in your whitetail hunting career is a 120 B&C class deer, then why not try to set your expectations at 140? I get a lot of clients who have harvested perhaps a 120 B&C deer as their best, and just because they're on a paid hunt they expect to come in and shoot a 170.

Looking at the credentials of the outfitter, in terms of client references, and asking a lot of questions regarding the morals and ethics of the outfitter, and picking up on what type of respect the outfitter has for the game—all these are important. I think all operators must have a deep regard for the wildlife in terms of how they manage the resource and how they feel about it. Another of the outfitter's important responsibilities is to appreciate the fact that the hunter has spent hard-earned money to come on this hunt. Additionally, he's taken vacation time. Nowadays time is so valuable to people and, when they book a hunt, they're looking for the experience of a lifetime. It's really a two-way street, so look for a guide who is cognizant of this.

Don White: Experience in the area where they hunt, and their success rate, are both important factors to consider. Checking as many references as you can is always important, too.

Eric Albus: Look for someone who's going to answer every one of your questions honestly. If he's too busy to answer your questions, he's too busy to go on a hunt with. Don't just go by references, because when you get references they will only be people who will give the outfitter a good recommendation. It does do some good to call references, but I think the most important thing is to spend time on the phone with the outfitter and make sure he's going to answer

A happy hunter and his big-woods prize. (Photo courtesy of Bill Honza)

all your questions. Never go with an outfitter who tells you only what you want to hear, either.

Keaton Kelso: Look for a guide who runs a professional business, and whose clients come back year after year. There are a lot of outfitters who are just good old boys, and they're hunters, but they're not businessmen. If you're going to spend the kind of money it takes to hunt whitetails in today's world, you ought to go with someone who runs a business. Knowing there's a businessman on the other end of the line when you're talking is so important when you're looking for an outfitter. It should also be somebody personable who knows his hunting grounds.

I'm also a firm believer in a totally guided hunt, rather than a semi-guided or unguided situation. After all, you're going to spend the money and you're going to travel, so your guide should be able to put you exactly where the bucks are likely to come out every day. This whole business runs on reputation, so it's a good idea to call around and get all the references you can.

James Woodley: A couple of things I'd suggest looking for: First, knowledge of deer, deer hunting, and all aspects of these; second, personality and being able to get along with people.

Gary Drinkall: In the whitetail business, it usually gets down ultimately to hunting private property. It really doesn't matter how good the deer country is, or how many big deer are there, if you can't get access to that land. You should really look at the outfitter's access to private land. Also, look at past clientele. You've got to look at how the guy's doing, and how many deer he's taking overall, and how many big deer he's taking. The whole key to keeping a good deer population is not killing any young bucks. If you run into an outfitter who's shooting the heck out of a bunch of 120-140 deer up in this country, you've got to be skeptical about that operation. But if the guy's killing some old age-class deer, even if they might not score that well, then the genetic pool is there and it's going to get better every year. If you want to kill a big deer, go with an outfitter who's trying to let his bucks mature fully.

Rene Semple: I'd have to say that the number one task in lining up a good guide is to find an ethical guy with ethical hunting practices. I'd look for an honest guy much more than one with a high success rate. I'd look for someone who has repeat hunters who haven't been successful, because that tells you that he runs a good operation, and people are having a good time. I'm looking at it from the other side of the fence, of course, but it doesn't always come down to how many animals you actually take, but rather the experience you have while you're in his camp.

Jim Shockey: Honesty, integrity, service, and quality are all important areas in assessing a guide's operation.

Duwane Adams: A hunter should look for an honest outfitter. If you get an honest outfitter, usually you'll get a square chance at killing a great buck. I'm sorry to say that in this business I think there are more dishonest outfitters than honest ones. That's just the way it is in America, not just with Coues deer outfitting but with outfitting in general. You want an honest outfitter, and if you've got that, I think you've got a great chance. You've just got to do your homework to find that honest outfitter.

Carlos Gonzalez Hermosillo: Experience is the best indicator of competence in a guide. Everyone is paying for service, and if there's experience, they should get it.

Kirk Kelso: The first thing you've got to check out is the outfitter's reputation. If he doesn't have a good one, there's a reason. A good outfitter should generate satisfied clients, and that's a great measure of how competent he is. Hunters also need to look into the quality of animals found in an area, and test it against their expectations. Are they looking for a good head or a really super one? If a guy's looking for a 160+ B&C deer, he should probably look at Canada. He sure wouldn't want to hunt, say, Florida, if that's his standard. If you want a big deer, you've got to go where the big deer live.

What is the most important single characteristic of a good guide?

Hal Blood: I'd say a good guide's most outstanding characteristic is being a person who gets along with people, because you're dealing with many different types.

Jeff Charles: Safety is the paramount consideration. If a guide's not safe out there, nobody is going to have a good time.

Dan Rosman: I'd say honesty and a good work ethic are tops. Another big thing is patience and the ability to relax and take it as it comes. It's good at times for a guide to be really gung-ho, but sometimes it's not very good for the hunter.

Choosing the right guide can mean the difference between success and a bad experience. (Photo courtesy of Bill Honza)

Chris Pevey: People skill is the most important one in my book. Even if the success isn't there, a person with people skills can show you a good time, and you can learn from him. A good guide should actually be forming a friendship with his hunter.

Charles Ruth: I think it's doing everything they can to treat all clients equally. You don't ever want to be in the situation where clients feel you're doing something more for one hunter than you are for another. Additionally, guides need to have real honesty and a good work ethic.

Jay Steen: I think you've got to be a people person to be a really outstanding guide. If you can't get along with your clients and don't go out of your way to please them, then it just won't work from the very start. A guide's got to have a good attitude and be willing to work with anyone.

David Davis: What I expect of a guide is for him to know what is representative of the area when a buck steps out. He's got to know his territory, so he can advise his hunter whether he can do better than that particular animal or not. He's also got to be able to hunt whitetails, and not everyone can do that.

Mike Gardner: I think the most important single characteristic is enthusiasm, and closely related to that is knowledge of the game in the area. As a guide, if you're not enthusiastic about your job, then you ought to be looking for a different line of work. The clients have taken hard-earned money, and valuable vacation time, and they're excited about the hunt. They need to be treated like you're aware of that and that you're doing your best for them. If you get up every morning to guide a client, then it's your job to be enthusiastic about it and to realize that this may be his trip of a lifetime. It may be the fourth or fifth client you've guided in the last month, but to him it's a trip he's waited for all year. If we're not enthusiastic for the clients, we ought to be doing something else.

Don White: A guide's most critical characteristic is a willingness to work hard for the client, because that's key to having a good hunt, and a good chance at taking a buck.

A truly good guide scouts the postseason to know what kind of bucks are still in the woods. (Photo courtesy of Bill Honza)

Eric Albus: Honesty.

Keaton Kelso: Knowing the ground and the deer that you're hunting. We spend numerous hours in the off-season glassing, knowing exactly how the deer are moving on our properties. A guide has got to know where the deer are moving and what they're feeding on at different times of the year.

James Woodley: I think consistency, not being late, and that kind of thing, are very important.

Gary Drinkall: Hard work is a real key. In my operation, the guides are the farmers and ranchers themselves, so they know the land already and they've got good hunting places. But as far as the individual guide goes, in addition to a knowledge of the land, he needs a good work ethic in trying to get his hunter an outstanding buck.

Rene Semple: Character is the most important attribute of a good guide, in my opinion. Attitude and drive and determination all come down to having good character.

Jim Shockey: The ability to hold a conversation with a diverse clientele is a major key to being an outstanding guide. It's affability, but it's really more than that, because you've got to be able to understand the client and be more than just a nice guy. You've got to understand what the client wants and then give that client the hunt he's looking for. Being nice is about 1 percent of what a guy needs to have, but there's a lot more to it than that.

Duwane Adams: For my kind of hunting, a major factor in being a good guide is being in great physical condition. We'll discuss this more later, but he also has to have the best binocular made, if that fits as a characteristic. The country is so demanding and brutal that it requires both of these.

Carlos Gonzalez Hermosillo: I'd again say experience is the most important factor.

Kirk Kelso: Knowledge of the animal you're hunting as well as knowledge of the area being hunted are very close together in importance.

What is the worst possible deficiency in a guide?

Hal Blood: I'd say laziness, but that's going to be a hard one for people to find out until they get there. There's just no excuse for laziness, and you just can't guide that way. You've got to give 110 percent to your clients all the time. This is especially true of the older guides. I'm not cracking down on the older guys, because I'll be older someday, too, but unfortunately I've found that a lot of them just don't have their heart in it anymore. And if that's the way they feel, they really should go find something else to do. I don't think people who are burned out are giving people their money's worth.

Jeff Charles: A guide's worst deficiency is when he refuses to put the deer in the background, focuses entirely on getting a deer, and essentially doesn't care about the needs of the guest hunter. You could see the buck of a lifetime and take off after it, and if you've got a guy who weighs three hundred pounds and smokes two packs a day, you just can't get away with that. Pretty soon the hunter is huffing and puffing and sweating, and when he's spent, you're done. You've got to be wise enough to tell the guy, "I think we can get that deer, but we've got to go at this a little differently."

Dan Rosman: Lack of communication skills is a big deficiency. Also, nobody wants to be around someone who's lazy and dirty.

Chris Pevey: The worst deficiency in a guide has to be poor people skills. When I hire a guide, if he doesn't have people skills, he doesn't last, because he just can't get along with hunters. Hunters expect a lot out of you, but if you can make it fun and exciting for them, they're going to have a good hunt, even if you have to turn a hunt into a nature walk. A person without people skills just can't do that.

Charles Ruth: Lack of preparation, and not demonstrating a willingness to work hard for the client, are both major deficiencies that will definitely be apparent to the client.

Jay Steen: The worst deficiency would be a lack of people skills. In addition, a good guide can't be deficient in knowledge of the area he's hunting or the deer that live there, or he just can't deliver.

David Davis: Being unable to age and score a whitetail on the hoof would be my pick of major deficiencies. However, I do tell people not to ask me what a deer will score while we're hunting, because if you tell them it's 140 and he turns out to be 139¾, they're not happy because you said he'd score 140!

Mike Gardner: Probably not being professional would come first on my list of guide deficiencies. My wife and I have been fortunate to travel and hunt in other parts of the country, and even in other parts of the world, and I always look to my guide to be professional in the way he conducts himself. I expect him to hunt hard with me, and to be enthusiastic and a true professional. He's got to be a good representative of the company he works for. The way I look at it, I might have my wife or my son along with me, and I look to my guide to be someone I can trust around my family. We're all there to hunt hard and have a good time, and to me it's the total experience of the hunt, the people you're with, what you see, and what you experience that makes the whole trip enjoyable. The guide is a tremendous part of that total experience factor and the enjoyment that comes from it.

Don White: In my experience, the worst deficiency has been the inability to judge a deer's age on the hoof. They've got to be able to properly age the deer, and a lot of guides will overestimate or underestimate the deer's age, as well as misjudge the antlers.

Eric Albus: Lack of integrity tops the list. All the guys I have guiding for me I'd trust with my wife and kids, my money, even my dog!

Keaton Kelso: I've had guys who worked for me who were hunters through and through, but they could not deal with a hunter client. They couldn't sit in a box stand and spend time with the hunter and make it an enjoyable experience. You can be the greatest hunter in the world, but if you don't have those personality skills you can't be a guide, because the guide has to make it a fun hunt for the client. It's not just putting deer in front of the client, but it's enjoying your job and interacting with the client, because you're not going to have deer in front of you all the time every day. People come on a guided hunt not just to kill an animal, but also to have a vacation. They want to have fun on that vacation and enjoy the day. People who enjoy the hunt will go back year after year to the same place, even if they've had no success, simply because they know the people, they're treated well, and they have a good time.

James Woodley: In my opinion the worst deficiency is dishonesty. You've got to be able to trust your guide.

Gary Drinkall: Laziness and drinking are two things to absolutely avoid, so I'd place them at the top of my list.

Rene Semple: Laziness, without a doubt, has to be the worst deficiency.

Jim Shockey: Insecurity is a major fault. If a guide feels insecure and thinks he has to prove that he's tougher in the

The buck of your dreams could be waiting if you do your homework in finding the right guide. (Photo by Bill Honza)

woods than the banker from New York who booked the hunt, that's an insecurity that results in the guide leaving the hunter in his wake attempting to prove that he's a better man. He's insecure about his own abilities, and he chooses to prove himself in ways in which the client can't compete, so it makes him feel like he's a bigger man. Insecurity can also stem from an inability to make a call on the quality of an animal.

Duwane Adams: They've got to be in top shape and have the right tools. If they don't have good equipment, and if they're not in good condition, then they can't give their all for you as a client, and that's an unforgivable fault. You're going to be robbed. If they've got discounted binoculars and weigh three hundred pounds, you're in deep trouble.

Carlos Gonzalez Hermosillo: Dishonesty tops my list of major deficiencies. With such a guide or outfitter, you can find yourself in the middle of nowhere, and only then do you find out that everything you were told isn't right. It has the makings of a disaster when dishonesty comes into play.

Kirk Kelso: The worst possible deficiency I see in any guide is the inability to relate to a client. If the guide has no personality, the client will not have a good time, no matter what he does in the way of hunting.

Chapter 3

THE WHITETAIL GUIDES EVALUATE THE HUNTER

What is your favorite type of hunter [personality, physical abilities, experience level, socioeconomic status, and so forth]?

Hal Blood: I like to have people in camp who are willing to learn because they'll listen to you. They're not know-it-alls, and they'll do what you say. I also like people who will take the time to get in shape and prepare for the hunt because if they don't, then you can't do what you need to do for them. If you're not in shape hunting in Maine, you're not going to be in a good position to do anything. You might go sit on a stump somewhere, but that's about all. I like to take people out who can adjust to the conditions, do some tracking, and whatever else it takes.

Jeff Charles: My personal favorite is someone who really enjoys the hunt itself. There are some people who want the trophy to hang on the wall, but they don't enjoy the hunt. I want the person who truly enjoys being out there and making lasting memories. As far as physical capabilities go, I have some guys who don't have that, and I have to put them in a stand and work with them that way, and that's fine, but they make up for their lack of physical ability because they *want* to hunt. I have other guys who are out with me for six days from morning to night, and they really get out there and go. If they're enjoying themselves, that's my kind of hunter.

Dan Rosman: A good personality and friendliness are near the top of my list. As far as physical ability goes, hopefully they can move around a little and be able to do some walking. Their ability determines how we're going to hunt. Experience level isn't very important, because sometimes a guy who doesn't have much experience is more fun to guide than someone who's been hunting all his life. The socioeconomic status doesn't matter, either, if

Safe firearms-handling in the field by the hunter is perhaps THE most important factor to most guides.

he's a person who simply enjoys life. I really like a person who's there just to savor the hunt.

Chris Pevey: I love a guy who's passionate about hunting. He's not there for the kill, and certainly not for the easy kill. I want him to enjoy the aesthetic value of the land we're hunting on, and to be able to see everything that I see: the view, the values, and the adventure of the outdoors.

Charles Ruth: That's a hard question for me to answer, and it shouldn't be, because I've dealt with the whole spectrum of hunter types. I guess if I had to nail down a single type, it would probably be the individual who is a regular guy who had to save up for the hunt, and it's the trip of a lifetime for him. I feel that type of person will really pay attention to you, listen to instructions, and be as patient as anyone while on the stand.

Jay Steen: I like a hunter who's in it for the experience more than for the kill, and comes in with the attitude that he'll have a good time when he gets here. That kind of personality is easy for us to accommodate.

David Davis: I like a blue-collar varmint hunter. He can shoot. He's worked a second job and scrimped and saved for the trip, and he appreciates a good deer when he kills one. Furthermore, he doesn't expect one automatically. Those people are great to guide. However, surprisingly enough, I can count on one hand the people I really didn't enjoy guiding. Part of that is that here we get a lot of pretty serious whitetail hunters, and they've been up and down the road more than once. But when you send me a virgin hunter, send me a blue-collar varmint hunter. He's excited about the hunt and it's going to mean something to him.

Mike Gardner: We're all there on a mission to hunt hard and find good game and harvest it, but I really enjoy clients with a good sense of humor and honest expectations. It's all too easy to get caught up in the thought that you're there just to harvest a big deer. You've got to remember that you're there to enjoy yourself, more than anything. I like a client who has come prepared, someone who's in shape and ready for the hunt. I enjoy guiding all types of people with the whole spectrum of different personalities, and I don't think that it's right to discriminate against people and expect that all types of people can be professional hunters. Clients are people with different abilities and personalities from differing walks of life, and you've got to realize that. I really enjoy having a client come in who's not so serious that he can't enjoy himself.

Don White: I always prefer the guy who saves his pennies all year and the time with me is his hunt of a lifetime. I like the construction worker, the guy who doesn't get to go on a high-dollar hunt very often, because he's willing to put 100 percent into the hunt.

Eric Albus: I like to take the guy who is here to enjoy the experience, and who realizes that hunting is about far more than killing something. I really appreciate the guys who come in and don't put any pressure on themselves or their guides to kill a deer. They've gotten past that level of having to kill to enjoy the hunt, and when they do harvest an animal it's just a bonus. My favorite hunter is the one who doesn't take himself or the hunt too seriously. It makes the hunt more enjoyable for everyone involved.

Keaton Kelso: I like a hunter who has some experience, but I don't like a hunter who knows everything about the hunt. My most enjoyable hunters are those with a lot of experience so they already know how to hunt whitetails. They'll sit in a stand without moving until 11:30 A.M., and then they'll go back to that same stand for the afternoon without complaining. They'll do it day after day simply because I've told them there are good bucks there. They understand that the big one isn't going to walk by them every day, and that it takes patience. They know that you can sit several days and not even see a deer, and then the next day a 180 B&C can step out.

As far as socioeconomic status goes, some of my best hunters are middle-class guys who have one vacation a year, and when they show up in camp they're helping to cut wood,

Guides must assess their hunters' abilities in order to give them the best chance of success. (Photo courtesy of Bill Honza)

helping to clean up, and so on, because they feel like they're just part of the group. Sometimes you get someone who's a multimillionaire, and a lot of them are really great people. But other times, with rich guys, you get them here and you have to baby-sit them simply because they're rich and they expect preferential treatment. On the other hand, some of the wealthy hunters pitch in and you can't tell how much money they've got; from their actions, you'd never know. I enjoy hunters who are willing to listen, because they know it's our property and that we know what's going on here. Physical ability really doesn't matter, because we can get a guy in a ground blind regardless of the shape he's in.

James Woodley: My favorite kind of guy is a middle-class type who's saved his money for a couple of years to be able to go hunting, and has really been looking forward to it. I like to do whatever I can to meet all his expectations and show him a good hunt. As far as physical abilities go, I'd prefer someone who's able to climb trees and get around a little, though we can accommodate almost anybody.

Gary Drinkall: To me the best hunter is one who's laid-back, has a good personality, and isn't pressuring you all the time. He can go with the flow and have a good hunting trip, not just a killing trip. I like the old-school hunters, because it was all about the hunt to them. If you're hunting a particular whitetail and you try to pattern that buck, and you're there giving it all you've got for a week or ten days, you might not happen to get a crack at him. My favorite type of hunter would still view that as a good hunt, because he realizes that simply doing everything right doesn't necessarily mean the buck will always cooperate.

Rene Semple: I like the guy who understands the hunt, and knows what hunting is really all about. I don't particularly like someone who's hunting for numbers. On the other hand, I appreciate someone who wants to experience a different part of the country and a different culture. I really like for a hunter to understand the concept of hunting, and good weather or bad, he always has a good hunt. That's the type of hunter we want, but it's not the type we always get, unfortunately.

Campfire revelry after a successful hunting experience. (Photo courtesy of Bill Honza)

Jim Shockey: The best hunters are the ones who come in with reasonable expectations. This means that they don't set up the guide or themselves for failure by looking for an animal that's impossibly big, looking for a hunt that can't possibly happen, or seeking an experience that's more of a dream than a reality.

Duwane Adams: I strongly prefer the guy who comes in and will listen to you right off the bat. If he'll listen to you, then you've got a guy who will do anything you tell him to do. Craig Boddington, even with his vast experience, falls into that category. Many times he and I have left at 2:00 or 3:00 A.M. and walked three or four hours in the dark with a flashlight. He wouldn't have a clue where I was taking him, but he believed that where we were going was exactly where we needed to be, so he followed without complaining. Almost always, when the sun came up, we'd be chasing big bucks. Some clients that come with you want to argue with you, and when you get someone who's argumentative, you're already off on the wrong foot. Also, physical conditioning is really important. If a guy arrives here and he's not in top condition, he's already set himself backward in trying to kill a big Coues buck.

Carlos Gonzalez Hermosillo: I prefer a hunter who is basically happy and stays in a good mood, one who can shoot well, and one who listens when the moment of truth arrives. It's easy to ruin a hunt when the hunter disobeys the guide's advice at the last moment. Then you have to do it all over again, and that's regrettable.

Kirk Kelso: My favorite type of hunter is the person who has a good attitude, and is there to enjoy the experience. That kind of person is a joy to have in camp. Those hunters get along with people in camp, and they're just good people to be around. I like a happy-go-lucky guy who's there to enjoy the experience of the hunt. If they're physically fit and they're able to handle the type of country they're hunting, it makes it that much better, but I'll take attitude over physical fitness. Any good guide can overcome a lot of deficiencies in the hunter, especially if the hunter has a good attitude.

What is the most challenging kind of hunter, and why?

Hal Blood: The biggest challenges are the ones who refuse to pay attention. They think they're just out on a nature walk, not a hunting trip. Sometimes I wonder why they come, because their mind's not in it, and I don't like it. I feel like I'm wasting my time, whether they feel like they're wasting theirs or not. It's no fun trying to do a good job for people and get them around a deer when they're not paying attention. They're fiddling around with something, or they're thinking about something else, or they're making a bunch of unnecessary noise.

Jeff Charles: I think the biggest challenge is the guy who won't listen to the guide. I've hunted my area for years, I know where the deer are usually located, and I'm pretty good at putting a guy on them. If a hunter thinks he knows more than I do, he might as well not hire me.

Dan Rosman: With me, it's score freaks who are the biggest challenge. The reason I say this is that they let so many nice animals walk by. Some people just let the score dictate the whole hunt. That kind of attitude can downright ruin a hunt. On a whitetail there are about sixteen different measurements, so it's really tough on the guide. I've seen a lot of guys let some really beautiful animals go by because the buck might not make 160 or 170 or whatever. That kind of stuff happens all the time, and everybody I've worked with here in Michigan says it's the biggest thing they don't like in hunters.

Chris Pevey: The biggest challenge to me is the hunter who must kill something at all costs. He puts a lot of pressure on you, because he's there only to kill something. Of course, everybody wants to harvest a deer, but that type of hunter is there for no other reason whatsoever, and you can't change them, so they are a real challenge to guide.

Charles Ruth: For me, the biggest challenge is the ultra-experienced hunter with an attitude. By that I mean he is the kind of person who continually reminds you of what he's done in hunting and what a good hunter he is. I love to hunt with experienced hunters, but I don't want to hear about their exploits all the time I'm with them. The experience they've had isn't the problem; it's the incessant discussion of what they've done in the past, and in effect talking down your own efforts to give them a good hunt.

Jay Steen: In this business, I think the most challenging hunter is one who has had to work and save to come on the trip, and he comes in expecting to automatically kill a deer in exchange for his hard-earned money. Hunters like that can sure put pressure on you to deliver, and they'd be better off going to a fenced game ranch with that attitude.

David Davis: The scoring system on whitetails can generate a real challenge for every guide in camp. Everybody sits around the fire the night before we hunt, and they hear this 150-160-170 nonsense, and usually they don't know one from a helicopter when they see it. I say this to point out that the most challenging type of hunter is the guy who has unrealistic expectations. He's watched it on television, and he hears these numbers, and he assumes that those deer are everywhere. One of the first questions I ask a guy when he gets in the truck the first morning is, "Other than the biggest deer on the ranch, what kind of deer would you like to kill?" Not that I can go out there and put my finger on that deer, but some guys like wide, some like heavy, some like multi-pointed deer, and if you can tell me that and I know where that kind of deer is located, you and I are going to go over there and spend a little time.

If the guy says all he wants to kill is a deer that scores 180 or better, I tell him to sit down because it's going to be a long hunt. He already asked all the right questions when he booked the hunt, but once he gets there he'll spring that on you. The amazing thing is that the first 140 that walks out in front of him, he nearly falls out of the stand! So he doesn't know, and if he did he might not need me.

Mike Gardner: As you well know, there are some hunters who are far too focused on killing a big deer. From the time they get here until the time they leave, they're so zeroed in on this

Would this deer give you buck fever? (Photo courtesy of Don White)

fact that they're not taking in what's going on around them. They don't enjoy the hunt, because the end is the focus rather than the experience. The hunter who has set his expectations so high in terms of game quality that he can't think of anything else is a real challenge to guide. There's a lot of press that comes out these days about trophy hunting and the record book, and that's a part of what we all do. But having clients come in who have their expectations set so high that they're just not enjoying themselves is distressing to me.

It's tough to be with a guy for several days when he's so uptight like that. You might have a client who's got his heart set on a 160-class deer, and you're in open-range, fair chase conditions, and you know that you have such deer there because you take them every year, but you also know that not everybody can get one. Maybe you're putting the hunter on some good deer in the 140s and 150s, and they're just so set on that benchmark that they're turning them down, and along with it they're missing a heck of an experience.

Don White: I took that question a little differently from most guys, I'd bet. For me, the most challenging hunter is the one who's willing to pass up multiple good bucks in order to try to find a truly great buck. That's the kind of challenge I enjoy. It's not a negative kind of thing but a positive, if you look at it that way.

Eric Albus: The most challenging guy is the one who isn't happy, no matter what. He's not even happy for his friends when they tag a nice buck. The guy who has to kill is the worst one to guide. And it's the guy who thinks he has all the answers, and knows more about the area than you do. He's continually second-guessing the guides, and it takes about twenty seconds for that to get old.

Keaton Kelso: The biggest challenge is the hunter who insists up front that he's a big trophy hunter and all he shoots is 180-class deer. I don't care where in the world you hunt whitetails, you don't kill that kind of deer every day. There's not a guy out there in a free-range operation who's shooting 180-class whitetails every week. For a client to expect that, he's talking to the wrong person when he talks to me. He needs to forget the experience part, and call a fenced operation somewhere and go buy a deer like that. That's probably my biggest pet peeve with hunters—expecting something that's not attainable unless you put in the necessary time. I appreciate a really good trophy hunter who says he's going to book five years in a row, because he knows there are B&C deer here on the property. He also is wise enough to know it's going to take that kind of time to kill one of them.

James Woodley: The ones who don't talk to you very much are a real challenge. They don't let you know what's going on in their heads. If they've got a problem with something, they should let you know so you can fix it.

Gary Drinkall: The biggest challenge to me is the guy who changes tires for a living, and he's had to borrow and scrape and save to pay for the hunt. You know he's done this in order to be able to be there, and you're really trying to get him something good. If you come up short, that's definitely the kind of guy you feel the worst about, because he can't afford a shutout.

Rene Semple: The greatest challenge is the guy who knows everything before he gets here and won't listen to you. Now, guides don't know it all, by any means, but we sometimes get guys who think they know more than we do. We live in the area, we hunt here all the time, and yet they're the ones who think they know where the deer are located.

Jim Shockey: The most challenging person is the hunter who's saved up all his pennies forever and ever, and he wants this hunt to be the hunt of a lifetime. It's almost impossible to live up to those expectations.

Duwane Adams: For me, it's not usually their attitude but their poor physical condition that makes them a challenge. If I get a guy who comes to hunt Coues deer, and he's over three hundred pounds, I know I've got a problem. I ask hunters like that if they've been walking a lot, and they all tell you they have been, and in fact they haven't walked farther than the refrigerator and the bedroom and the garage in ten years. You cannot hunt big Coues bucks, any way in the world, unless the hunter can do what you tell him. If he's out of shape, it's just impossible for him.

The kill is the culmination of a string of careful choices—chief of which may be following your guide's instructions.

Carlos Gonzalez Hermosillo: For me, the biggest challenge is guiding the ladies. Most of them are tougher and can shoot better than the men, but they expect you to be better than their husbands in a lot of ways. They are lovely, but they can have very high expectations of their guide, more so than most men. They judge you much differently than the guys do, and they expect 110 percent from you. That's fine, but it can make the guide feel like he must be Superman, and that's tough. Not that we don't like guiding the ladies, because we do, but you're asking me what kinds of hunters are challenging, and the ladies certainly are.

Kirk Kelso: The most challenging type of hunter to me is the one who thinks he already knows everything, yet knows nothing. The know-it-all hunter isn't likely to listen to his guide.

How do you handle the inexperienced hunter? The physically challenged hunter?

Hal Blood: The truth is that the way I hunt, I'm not able to take anyone who's physically challenged. I will send them out with one of my other guides because they're the ones who are going to be sitting on a stand or posted up somewhere. I don't guide people in that category because it's just not the way I hunt. Inexperienced is OK, though. I'd just as soon take somebody who doesn't really know much about it as long as he's willing to learn.

Jeff Charles: As I said before, safety is my biggest concern, whether a person is experienced or not. On the first day the hunters are here, usually on Sunday when we can't hunt, I like to take them out to the range and see how safely they handle the firearm. That way, I know how safe I'm going to be, as well as everybody else in the area, when those people are around with a firearm. From that perspective, I adjust to the client. If it's somebody I have to watch, I'll be on him all the time. On the other hand, if I feel he's comfortably safe, then I'll be more relaxed.

Now, as far as handicapped hunters are concerned, it goes back to that first day they come into camp, when I have to assess them to determine their capabilities. A person who is physically handicapped, say in a wheelchair, is put on a stand. We can usually predict when the deer will be coming by with the highest level of probability. If people can't stay on stand all day long, we put them out during the optimum times and bring them in for the other times. Maine is one of the toughest states to hunt in, I can tell you, with a lot of cutovers and blowdowns, and we hunt at elevations between 1,100 feet and 2,600 feet. You really have to be in shape to hunt well in such areas, but we do take handicapped hunters and we have some success with them.

Dan Rosman: You've got to be as patient as you can be in both cases. For the inexperienced hunter, try to make it as much fun as possible, but watch the way he handles his rifle. I was almost shot once. You have to be patient because inexperienced hunters ask a lot of questions. It can be almost like guiding a little kid because it's "why and when and how" all the time. The physically challenged hunter requires the guide to be even more patient. I've had several hunters in wheelchairs, and it's always a tough deal that requires more than average persistence.

Chris Pevey: With the inexperienced hunter, I try to use the hunt as an instruction opportunity. I go into detail about everything, and think things through with him. I tell him why we're doing things, and I go out of my way to be very explanatory. With the physically challenged hunter, I do the same because I want him involved in the hunt. We've had some quadriplegics come in to hunt, and they're the best hunters you could possibly get, because they're just happy to be there. When these guys come on board, we have the hunts set up for them. We go into more detail in getting there early and getting everything set up right. It takes weeks to get such a hunt prepared so that everything goes smoothly, and it's a very challenging operation.

Charles Ruth: I have a lot of familiarity with inexperienced hunters, especially kids, and a good number of females, and a few men as well. The key to good success with them is that they don't have a lot of misconceptions or preconceptions about what you're going to tell them to do. They will follow your instructions, and I've found that if you can get them to shoot properly and to be comfortable with the weapon, they're going to do very well.

I don't have as much experience with disabled hunters, but I've dealt with some, and I'd say pretty much the same thing about them. If a person is truly disabled and he's gone to the trouble to get to the place to hunt, he's going to listen to what you tell him and do what he needs to do to make the hunt come to fruition. In all the handicapped cases I've dealt with, the clients come familiar with their weapons and ready to hunt. They want to go that extra mile, they're willing to sit as long as anybody else in camp, and they normally do very well.

Jay Steen: Experience level isn't important, as long as they've mastered gun safety. That's where we start with our hunters. We then try to educate them on how they're going to be hunting, and we explain the local rules to them, whether it's point restrictions or whatever. They're usually the easiest ones to guide, because they're aware that they don't know a lot. Most inexperienced hunters are more willing to listen to you, and do what you ask them to do, than some people with a lot of experience.

We don't have a lot of disabled hunters here, but we are certainly set up for them. With most truly disabled people who want to hunt, you don't even notice they're disabled, because they have a bad heart or something that isn't obvious. If they're in a wheelchair, we have ground blinds set up for them. It's funny, but most handicapped people don't really need extra attention except for a special blind or something like that. Sometimes, depending on the disability, you have to go and be there with them personally to provide whatever assistance they need.

David Davis: The inexperienced hunter is one of my favorites. Give me a few hours with him, and I can make a shooter out of him. Then we can go kill a deer. I love an inexperienced hunter because he's not as calloused and he gets excited over anything that walks out that's got a little class to it. You get a chance to explain young deer and old deer, to teach a little bit. Some of these other guys show up thinking they already know that. I love the inexperienced hunter because you tell him to hook his finger in your belt loop and come on, and you'll take him hunting. With the physically challenged hunter, here are my thoughts: If I ever get in the position of being unable to go because of age or physical

Are you patient enough to stay on the stand for hours in subfreezing conditions in order to bag your buck? (Photo courtesy of Hal Blood)

disability or anything else, I'd sure want somebody to take me hunting. I don't mind taking them at all, because it's worth it, in my opinion. Some guides will almost refuse to take the people with serious handicaps, and that's a shame.

Mike Gardner: My guides are all trained and encouraged to have a lot of patience. We all like to think we're professional guides and professional hunters, but what we all need to remember is that we were all novices at one time. It's intimidating enough for a hunter to travel all the way across the country and come into a camp where he's surrounded by professional hunters. That's what we do for a living. I always encourage our guides to treat all our clients with a lot of support and patience. The guides are here to make the trip a fun experience, and the client should really have no insecurities or embarrassment about being a novice. Every one of us has been one, too. We're still novices when we go to other parts of the world to hunt. If a guide wants to live in a glass house and think that everyone who comes to the camp who doesn't know as much as he does is somehow inferior, then he makes a huge mistake by looking down on them. We try to teach the opposite to our guides and encourage them to be very welcoming and open with our clients.

In south Texas we have a moderate climate with many roads and good access, so we're able to accommodate more when it comes to the physically challenged hunter than is the case in many places. When a vehicle can be used to get into a hunting area, it's a great help. It's not uncommon for two of our guides to pick up a wheelchair and lift it right into a deer stand or blind, then help the client into the stand. We don't do a lot of physically difficult walking in our type of hunting. Our area down here is relatively flat, though we do walk and rattle and that sort of thing, but we also do a lot of stand hunting, and in this type of environment you can accommodate the handicapped very well.

Don White: The guides and I will bend over backwards to initiate the inexperienced hunter into the whitetail world. For the physically challenged individual, all of us will do whatever we have to do to ensure success—put him in a ground blind instead of a tower, let him hunt out of the truck, whatever it takes.

Eric Albus: Inexperienced hunters are probably the most fun to guide. Those guys have guides up on a pedestal, and they believe everything we tell them, so they follow instructions. You can have more fun with them than with anybody else. We do spend a lot of extra time with such hunters, making sure they understand how, where, and what we're doing, and how we want to go about it. With them, and with the physically challenged, we assess their abilities and try to work within those abilities. Truly handicapped hunters require more planning, and it's definitely different, but they're usually patient and cooperative, and we just mold the hunt around their strengths. We've always prided ourselves on getting a good animal for handicapped hunters.

Keaton Kelso: I enjoy inexperienced hunters, but I can't put them in the woods without a guide. People do an unguided or semi-guided hunt and put the inexperienced hunter out there all alone, and that's wrong. If I do that and put him in one of my best areas, I won't be able to hunt that area again for probably a month, just because he can't be still, he's getting out of the stand, and so on, and it completely messes up an area. When we have inexperienced hunters, we're constantly with them, as if they're hooked to our sides 24/7. You pretty much have to walk them through the steps on how to kill a big deer. For the physically challenged, we have our setup pretty well arranged to accommodate all levels of physical ability. A lot of people come in who can't walk more than a couple of hundred yards, and can't climb at all. We have ground blinds set up for them, and we can drive right up to them.

James Woodley: You try to teach the inexperienced hunter what's going on and what to do. You have to show him a little bit about the whole experience and what he should be getting out of it. We have had a few physically challenged hunters in the past, even a few who were in wheelchairs, and we were able to set up ground blinds and they had a good hunt. They require a little extra attention, but that's no big deal. You can use a crossbow in Illinois if you have a handicap permit, and we've had at least one guy do that. A couple of them used shotguns with slugs, which are legal here.

Gary Drinkall: For inexperienced hunters, you've just got to explain things well. They need to know why you put a tree stand there, why you have a bait station there, why you've got a food plot there, why your stand is downwind, why you use this stand only in the morning and that one only in the evening, and so on. You've got to be descriptive and patient with them. As for the physically challenged hunter, again, you've got to talk it out with him, and he's got to realize how tough it is on the guide to try to pull this off. There will be days when you're going to have a tough time putting a physically challenged hunter in the right stand at the right time. Also, there may be a situation where he can't hunt the really good stand in the morning because he can't sneak in for half a mile to reach it.

Rene Semple: We've had both, and we usually wind up spending more time with them. We sometimes have to designate a guy to sit on the stand with them, rather than letting them sit alone. For the inexperienced hunter, it's a matter of helping him judge the deer, and for the physically challenged it's sometimes that, and sometimes it's just being there to help with physical needs.

Jim Shockey: The first thing is, you assign them guides who are far more patient than average. Second, you work with them within their abilities. Don't ask them to try to make a 300-yard shot that may or may not give them a bad experience. You gently ease them into a hunt within their capabilities. You try to assure them of a successful experience within the terms of reference of that particular hunt. You shouldn't try to push them beyond their capabilities for your own reasons, or for some reason of their own, where they're not capable of doing what's needed. For the special-needs client, you deal with him on a case-by-case basis. If someone's blind, you take him to where you can direct the barrel so that he can make his shot. If handicapped hunters have no legs, you just work within that capability. You're obviously not going to take them on a five-mile hike if they have no legs. If a person is deaf, you could do that, no problem, so you work within the capabilities of the individual hunter. We've taken hunters

Proficiency with the weapon is paramount when the big moment finally arrives. (Photo courtesy of James Woodley)

who in fact had no legs, and we had no problems getting them an animal. Anyone can hunt whitetails with me, and in my hunting territory we can handle almost any handicap.

Duwane Adams: The inexperienced hunter is generally not a big problem, because he'll most often listen to you. The physically challenged hunter, though, makes it very, very difficult. Because of the nature of our hunting country, its sheer brutality, it simply won't give you any chances at a good buck if you can't get around in it. You have to be in good physical shape or you're just not going to make it to where the big bucks are located.

Carlos Gonzalez Hermosillo: You have to be very patient with people who are inexperienced. You can't teach them everything in two or three days, so you just have to be patient. We've had some physically challenged hunters, too, and they have my utmost respect. They are really good people, the very best. Some of them do things that seem impossible to me. They love it, though, and it's a real challenge for us to set them up. We use vehicles a lot with them. A good area is very important when hunting with them. The Coues deer is extremely wary and doesn't like to get within shooting distance of a truck, but we try to do it because handicapped hunters deserve the extra effort on our part.

Kirk Kelso: I handle the inexperienced hunter just like I do my own children when they start hunting. You start them out by elaborating more on the experience to be had, rather than highlighting the harvest of an animal. Make sure that they're entertained the entire time. Hunting can be pretty boring at times, and if you can just keep them occupied and into the experience, you can create a situation where they're more apt to want to do it again. I like guiding women and young people, because they want to listen and learn. As for the physically challenged hunters, we meet their needs as best we can. I think the most important thing is to handle them on a one-on-one basis just like you do everyone else. By this I mean you don't point them out, you don't single them out, you don't cater to them more than you do the other clients. Make them feel like they're a part of the group and not somebody who's different.

Camp situations can test the hunter's ability to work with others and get along, especially in remote locations. (Photo courtesy of Hal Blood)

What type of hunter do you most dislike guiding? Is there any particular characteristic that would make you refuse to guide a hunter?

Hal Blood: Yes, I've had some I'd refuse to guide again. Usually it's the ones who are discourteous and disrespectful, and who don't fit into the camp life at the lodge. I call them the odd men out. Usually they are the ones who don't want to listen to anyone else because they already know everything. You've seen those individuals. When they start talking, people roll their eyes.

Jeff Charles: I most dislike it when a person does three things: disregards safety rules, starts drinking at noon, and won't abide by state laws. For example, we have a hunter orange rule up here, and if one of my clients goes in wearing hunter orange and comes out without it on, he's done. To me, hunting is so enjoyable, but it has to be safe, and if somebody isn't safe, it isn't fun. I'd refuse to guide anyone who persisted in practicing any one of these three things.

Dan Rosman: I've never refused to guide a hunter. I've come close a couple of times when hunters were really careless with the rifle, I guess. Every one of our clients goes to the range with us, even if he claims to be the best shot in the world. I do that mainly so I can watch how these hunters handle the rifle, and not so much to see if they can hit the bull's-eye. You've got to let them know we're not going to do it their way if it's unsafe. It all boils down to the ones who won't listen to you. When I first started guiding, I'd sometimes be taking out a fellow in his fifties; he would not listen to a young guide, and that made it tough.

Chris Pevey: I most dislike guiding a guy who's just got to kill something. He's there for one reason only, and he has no appreciation for the aesthetics of the hunt, the property, or the animal. He's there to pull the trigger and get his money's worth only in that way. I call such people trigger-happy, kill-thirsty hunters. They put tremendous pressure on you, of a kind that's extremely unpleasant. I also don't like a client to try to guide the guide, and some of them will if you'll let them.

Charles Ruth: I'd say it would be any hunter who refuses to follow instructions, particularly those related to safety. In my book, that can get you out of my camp pretty quick.

Jay Steen: Safety is so important. A hunter who isn't safe, and who is obviously a danger to the guides or to or other clients, would be someone I'd refuse to take. Also, if hunters won't go along with your game management program, and if they want to violate some aspect of it every time they come, you might want to refuse them.

David Davis: I simply will not take a hunter who is not safe. We have certain safety criteria that we follow as regards handling guns in the truck, how they're handled in camp, and so on. Basically, here we leave the guns in the truck from the time the hunters get here until they leave. Life's too short to hunt with a person who's unsafe.

Mike Gardner: I'd refuse to guide a hunter who's unsafe. We've got an orientation we give to clients when they get to camp, and it's to the effect that all the guides have families that we want to go home to at the end of this hunt. Quite frankly, it's just not worth it to be unsafe. There's no deer big enough to start compromising anyone's safety. It takes away from the enjoyment of the hunt if you're constantly looking over your shoulder to make sure they have their safety on and aren't pointing a gun at you. If a hunter is disrespectful in terms of safety, then I simply refuse to guide him. We don't need the income so badly that it's worth putting up with the prospect of getting someone hurt or killed.

Don White: I most dislike guiding hunters who have a preset score they've got to have. They say something like, "I've got to have a 160." When you're trying to judge the deer on the hoof, they're asking over and over, "What will it score, what will it score?" In my opinion it really doesn't matter—if you like the deer, shoot it! If not, we'll try to find you another one. People who are just hung up on B&C scores are a real pain to guide. I'd refuse to guide a hunter who handled a gun unsafely because he can injure you or kill you outright. In our case, any injury is serious because we're about fifty miles from the nearest hospital.

Eric Albus: The guy who must kill something is the kind I most dislike guiding. I'd refuse to guide anyone who demonstrated that he was unsafe, particularly with firearms. If I feel a person is a threat to himself, to me, to my guides, or to my staff, I won't hesitate to terminate the hunt.

Keaton Kelso: I can't stand a hunter who's a know-it-all. This person comes into my camp and my situation, he's never even been to Kansas before, and he's going to show me how to hunt. It's like a person coming onto your land and telling you that he knows where your 170 is, saying, "Just let me go hunt." It's ignorance at best for a person to think he knows more than the guides. You tell people to stay put on the stand, and you come back a few hours later and they're down and gone, and you find them in a ditch a few hundred yards away. They just walked right through the bedding area and they didn't even know it. When you're paying for someone to put you on a good deer, it's just common sense to shut up and do what he says.

As for refusing to guide a hunter, I'd refuse to guide someone who's being illegal or unsafe. If you're going to insist on doing either, there's the road. I also won't tolerate any rude, crude comments, because my wife and my mother are doing the cooking. If anyone is ruining the camp for the other hunters, I will tell him that either he straightens up or I'm taking him to the airport today. All the other hunters are there on vacation, and I can't let one individual ruin their experience.

James Woodley: Like I said before, I don't like guiding people who won't talk to you and won't communicate. I don't know if I'd ever refuse to guide a person, unless he was doing something totally off the wall, like breaking the law or going entirely against what you're telling him to do.

Gary Drinkall: We've always had problems with guys who are pushy, especially with their money. That really turns me off. I had one guy tell me, "I know how you guys work, so here's the deal: 'X' amount of dollars for this size animal, 'X' amount of dollars for that size." Of course that didn't go over very well with me. Also, those guys who think they're smarter than the guide irritate me to no end, especially when they're hunting in my country. I won't guide a guy again if he won't listen to me. You get a guy who comes in thinking he's smarter than you, and he has a good hunt anyway and books the next year. When he returns, he's ten times worse because now he actually does know a little about the country. If that attitude becomes intolerable, that's where I might just cut it off.

Rene Semple: I'd have to say I don't like guiding the guy who doesn't appreciate the hunt or the animal, and is hunting strictly to put an animal in the book. We love so much just to be out hunting, and they really don't even like being out with us in beautiful hunting country. They just want to get that animal and go. Furthermore, when they do shoot an animal, the first thing they want to do is put a tape to it, and I really don't like that. As for refusing to guide a hunter, if I've had them in before or talked with them at a show, and I'm sure they're like I'm describing, I'd refuse them.

Jim Shockey: As for anyone who's an unethical hunter or who is disrespectful to the animals in any way, I will refuse to

Paying attention to your guide and following his instructions can lead to the buck of a lifetime! (Photo courtesy of Don White)

guide him or outfit for him. It's not a question of disliking guiding such people; I just won't have them in my camps.

Duwane Adams: It's hard to see the characteristics you're talking about until you actually get the hunter into camp. The overbearing kind of person is a big problem because he can't get along with anybody. I'm not just talking about the guides, either; I mean the other clients. If a person is ill-mannered and disrespectful to other people, I can't take that. I teach my guides all the time to be as respectful of others as they would like to be respected.

For example, if you're from Georgia, and if a guy from New York or somewhere comes in and makes a big deal of talking about kicking your butt in the Civil War, how much of that are you going to take? Not very much, I'd wager. Well, let me tell you, I've had that very thing happen! It's a really abrasive form of disrespect. I've had to tell such people, "You know what? Your hunt's over!" I don't have time for disrespectful people. Generally, when I bring my tone of voice to that level, the crap stops because they know I mean it. I can take a guy who's inexperienced or a guy who's overweight and out of shape; it's a handicap, but it's not a big deal. It's just the cards you're dealt, and you just go along with them and do the best you can. But people who are ill-mannered are the worst kind of hunters, because they're really the worst kind of people.

Carlos Gonzalez Hermosillo: I don't like arrogant people. I once had a prince come to hunt with me, and I just could not treat "His Royal Highness" like he expected. I had to take him back to the airport two days after he got here, and I gave him his money back and told him, "Listen, bye-bye, you're just not my type of client." Arrogance is the worst thing I can think of in a hunter. Everybody's money is as good as the next person's, and it doesn't matter if it's a prince's money or just an ordinary guy's, it's all the same to me. If I can avoid the arrogant hunter, then I don't have to suffer!

Kirk Kelso: The ones I don't like to guide are those who always seem to be in a hurry. They get here, they're rushing, they're on their cell phone all the time, they want to get their animal killed as quickly as possible, and then they want to put pressure on everyone to get them back to the airport so they can get out. That's not the kind of client I like to guide. To me, they're into hunting for the wrong reasons. Clients I would refuse to guide are the ones who are incompetent with their firearms to the point where they pose a danger to others. Another thing that might cause me to refuse a client would be if he treated the employees, the guides, or even the cooks and camp help, with disrespect.

What is the worst thing a client can do on a hunt?

Hal Blood: There are a lot of bad things clients can do, but one of my pet peeves is drinking too much. I don't like it when people come on a hunt just to drink a lot. I won't allow them to drink while we're out hunting, of course, but when they're back here some of them tend to drink way too much at night. In remote camp, we control it, because lights are out at 8:00 P.M.; here, however, the clients can be up half the night playing cards and drinking, and they aren't going to be ready to hunt the next day.

Jeff Charles: The worst thing they can do is abuse the game laws or the rules of safety. If a person becomes unsafe, or violates the game laws, it's pretty bad. I had a guy shoot a doe on purpose once, illegally, and naturally he wasn't in camp the next day. I tell my clients that if they break the law, I'm going to call the game warden. My license means too much to me to risk losing it.

Dan Rosman: Poor shooting in general is a bad deal, as is shooting at animals that they shouldn't be trying to take. Also, if they wound an animal, I hate it when they act like they just don't care.

Chris Pevey: I think the worst thing a client can do is to try to guide the guide. Never guide the guide, because guiding is the guide's job! I meet with my guides all the time, and I always tell them, "Don't let them guide you!"

Charles Ruth: To me, the worst thing is failing to follow instructions, particularly related to safety.

Jay Steen: Not paying attention to the guide is the biggest pitfall. This is especially true the way we hunt because we have to tell the clients pretty much what to expect and what to do. For example, we tell them to sit in one place and stay put. If they refuse to listen and want to do the opposite of what the guide tells them, they're not helping themselves. Some guys want to guide themselves when they come, and then they want to blame their guide because they weren't successful!

David Davis: The worst thing is to miss when they get a legitimate opportunity. And close behind that is to not sit still. On the missing, it's just six seconds out of four days, because there's a mere six-second window of opportunity on a good hunt. Don't goof it up!

Mike Gardner: Being disrespectful to our staff and acting in an unsafe manner are the most serious offenses. We've had very, very few clients we've had to carry to the front gate and ask them to leave the ranch because they were disrespectful to our staff, but that's probably the worst case. Everyone on our staff is trained to help our clients have a good time and an enjoyable hunt. They're the clients, they've spent the money, and we're there for them. By the same token, we also like to have that mutual respect.

Don White: The worst thing would be to shoot the guide! Significantly short of that, it's not listening to what the guide has to say. Another thing is when they're not truthful about their hunting or shooting abilities, because we need to know the real story about these things, since it affects how we approach their hunt. We need to know their capabilities with the firearm.

Eric Albus: It's bad when the hunters put too much pressure on themselves and their guides to kill something, and also when they compromise safety for any reason.

Keaton Kelso: Not listening to the guide is pretty bad, and also not taking the professional advice they're being given. I see it every day. I might tell my clients to sit on particular stands until ten o'clock, and at 8:00 A.M. I drive by and they'll be sitting at the side of the road. I can tell them firmly not to get out of their tree stands, and in extreme cases the first thing they do is get down. Their professionals are telling them exactly what they have to do to kill a trophy, and they're doing the total opposite.

There are plenty of guys out there who book hunts with qualified guides, and they have no idea how to hunt whitetails on their own. They're constantly moving, reaching in and out of their packs, smoking on the stand, and so on. The techniques that work in your home area to kill 110-class bucks just won't work when you're trying to kill a 180-class buck. If you aren't doing everything your guide tells you, all you're going to see is the smaller bucks. The big, mature ones just are not going to show up in your field of vision. Actually, for about 95 percent of our clients who kill big bucks, it's because we're on the stand with them to make sure they do everything right. When they're alone, they're doing stupid things that keep the big guys away.

James Woodley: For bowhunting, as with most of our hunts, the worst thing would be getting down and walking around instead of staying put.

Gary Drinkall: Insulting you by trying to buy you is very offensive. A few hunters apparently think that you're for sale and that you're not going to work for them unless they flash some money in front of your face.

A wall full of wall-hangers is the payoff for the hunter who listens best and persists longest. (Photo courtesy of Jeff Charles)

Rene Semple: Breaking the law, or violating hunting ethics in some way, would probably be the worst things a hunter could do.

Jim Shockey: To wound an animal and then laugh about it, like it's funny, is a grievous offense by any hunter.

Duwane Adams: The worst thing they can do is not pay attention to you. I had a guy get lost because he didn't listen to me, and it took me all day to find him. I had told the guy to sit on a rock and wait for me for a few minutes, and he took it on himself to go one ridge farther over. I didn't get a hundred yards from where I left him, and when I came back he wasn't there. Why hire a guide if you're not going to listen to him? You can get into life-threatening situations here, because that guy didn't have a clue how to get back to the truck. Today some hunters will have a GPS, and that's better, but in the old days especially it wasn't a piece of cake. Even with a GPS it's dangerous to go wandering off on your own in the kind of country I hunt.

Carlos Gonzalez Hermosillo: On a group hunt, like most deer camps, I think the worst thing a hunter can do is bring all his problems to the rest of the group. The other hunters don't deserve that, because they're there to have fun, and we all have some kinds of problems. If there are any problems at all with the hunt, they try to blame everything on the guide. They'll say, "Oh, I shot this one, but it was running away, and I couldn't see the antlers . . ." And they're complaining, even though they killed a good animal. Such an attitude can infect the rest of the group and make it less enjoyable for them.

Kirk Kelso: The worst thing they can do is to not listen to the professional they've hired to do a job for them. If a guide is a professional, and if he's done his homework, the hunter needs to listen and let the guide's magic and expertise work on the animal he wants to kill.

Chapter 4

THE WHITETAIL GUIDES EVALUATE HUNTING ARMS

What is your favorite rifle caliber for whitetails? What caliber do you recommend for clients?

Hal Blood: My favorite caliber is the .30-06, but I tell hunters to bring whatever they're comfortable shooting. I do recommend they bring something from .270 on up, because up here we have bigger-bodied deer. They don't need a .300 magnum to hunt here, but something on the order of a .308 or a .30-06 is perfect.

Jeff Charles: In our country, I like to see someone with a heavy bullet, at least 180 grains, so I lean toward the heavier calibers. I personally shoot a .350 Remington Magnum. I also have a short-action .300 magnum. Anything that has a big bullet, even a slow-moving big bullet, is preferable. We have some clients come with a .25-06, which is great for stand hunting down South, but when you're looking at a 250-pound deer, that bullet may not kill the deer quickly enough for you to recover it. If a guy has several rifles, I tell him to bring the one that he feels most comfortable shooting and can shoot best. If it's someone who's a little afraid of bigger guns, a .308 is perfect for that person, and so is a .30-06.

The hunter doesn't have to shoot a giant wildcat magnum to kill a deer, because then he's going to flinch, and he's going to miss. For kids, I'll tolerate a 7mm-08, even though the bullet weight is only 140 grains. I'd avoid the .243, because I think it's the worst deer rifle ever made. But you've got to be comfortable with what you're shooting. I had one guy switch from a .308 to a .300 magnum, and he was afraid to shoot it! He was better off with the .308! I'm not big on speed, because up here bullet weight is more important in order to get through the brush and into the vitals.

Dan Rosman: I've always liked the .300 Winchester Magnum, and that's what I recommend for clients. You can load them up with a little bit heavier or a little lighter bullets. You hunt some of these big northern deer, and you'll find that they're a really stout animal. We've shot deer here in Michigan that weighed 356 pounds, and that's a big animal. I tell my clients to bring at least a .270. Another great deer rifle is the 7mm magnum.

Chris Pevey: My favorite is the .25-06. It's a great caliber because it will reach out there far enough, but you don't have it in your brain that you can make a four- or five-hundred-yard shot. It's pretty much limited to three hundred yards or so, so you don't even think about making such a shot, and that's advantageous where we hunt. It's a deadly caliber for short-range shooting, and it doesn't kick at all, so anyone can shoot it without flinching. I also like the .270 and the .30-06. In southern Georgia, where we hunt, these guns are proven performers. If you have a gun that can do more than you can do, it will sometimes get you in trouble, because you'll try shots that you shouldn't attempt. For clients I uniformly recommend something that they feel comfortable and confident shooting.

Charles Ruth: I actually have quite a bit of scientific experience with this. I did a study using a sample size of five hundred hunters, and I was on the ground there dealing with the deer, including the misses, the hits, and so on. For each shot, I recorded the type of weapon and the type of bullet used, and any other pertinent information. The bottom line is that I recommend the caliber that the hunter is comfortable using, because my research indicates that the performance of a .243 and that of a .300 magnum are identical statistically. Keep in mind that we're in the Southeast and we've got relatively small deer here, but what this means in our area is that the hunter should use what he's most comfortable shooting.

When I see a guy break out a .243 or a 6mm or a .257, I'm all for it because I know he's already been through the flinching with the larger calibers and has settled on a rifle that's right for him. Understand, I'm not saying the larger calibers are bad, but what I'm looking for is a hunter on the range who's drilling the target time after time with no flinching. What this means is that I can recommend any caliber at all, as long as the hunter is comfortable with it and can shoot it well.

Jay Steen: I don't really have a favorite. The .270 and .30-06 always stand out as very good deer rifles in our terrain and with our conditions. These calibers are so common that if your ammunition doesn't show up or you forget it or something, you can go to any sporting-goods store and buy some, it's so available. For clients I recommend anything .25-06 and above. A lot of people start youngsters out with a .243 just for the reduced recoil, and they're great guns from that standpoint, but you just don't have enough of an exit wound on a bad shot to follow up by tracking the deer. There's nothing more discouraging than for a kid to have an opportunity to harvest his first deer, and it runs off and can't be found for lack of an adequate blood trail.

David Davis: The .300 Winchester Magnum shooting a 180-grain bullet. I will not allow anything less than a .270 in any of our camps. We need a killing shot right on the spot, because where we hunt you've got to have a bulldozer to find the animal if he goes thirty yards off into the brush. In my opinion, there's no such thing as overkill. You need a bullet hole that goes all the way through and leaves a hole on both sides. I gear my hunters up for the worst-case scenario; I rattle up a big buck and he's suddenly walking away, and a guy's got to shoot him from behind. If he's got a good bullet in the right gun, he's going to get thirty inches of penetration, and get up there where he lives. Of course, standing up broadside, you can shoot them down all day long and they'll roll over and die. Naturally, for my clients I recommend the .300 Winchester Magnum, if they can shoot it.

Mike Gardner: My favorite is the .30-06. My dad bought me a Weatherby .30-06 when I was about fourteen, and I've got the old Leupold 3X9 variable, and it's still my favorite gun. We do have a lot of clients nowadays who bring Remington 7mm Magnums, and those seem to do really well, being a flat-shooting gun with a lot of knockdown power. For clients I'd recommend either. Some clients come in with .300 Winchester Magnums,

A bipod is favored by many guides for long shots.

and that's a little heavy, in my opinion. Anything below a .243 is much too light, I think.

Don White: You want to know my favorite caliber right now? It changes, you know. Right now it's the 7mm magnum. I hunted with a 7mm STW for years and wore my barrel out completely. I sent it out to get it rebarreled, and went to the 7mm magnum. On our ranch, I recommend any magnum, because our deer are really tough. They live in cactus and thorns, and it takes a pretty good hit to kill them. Generally, with a magnum, even if it's a marginal hit, it helps with tracking them. I've seen them suck up smaller bullets and that's it, they're gone.

Eric Albus: I like the .30-caliber magnums, because our whitetails are larger and can be tough to put down. Superior bucks seem to have a superior will to live, as well. I use Robert Ruark's advice, "Use enough gun." For clients I recommend anything they can shoot well, because it's still true that bullet placement is far more important than the caliber you're using, even on a big whitetail. If that gun is a .243, we work hard to keep the shots less than 150 yards. I prefer the .270 as the minimum caliber, though, and I feel a serious trophy caliber starts with the 7mm Remington Magnum.

Keaton Kelso: For Kansas and Nebraska, my favorite is the .300 Weatherby Magnum. In our country it's not unusual to take three- to four-hundred-yard shots. The guys who are killing bucks at that range are killing them with that rifle. The 7mm magnum also works well for long shots. In Missouri, the .270 or the .30-06 is a good choice, because we're hunting more wooded terrain and the shots tend to be closer. For clients I recommend these rifles, but I stress that they should be comfortable with the rifle.

James Woodley: I'm so much into bowhunting that I'm not very experienced with rifles. We can hunt with slugs in shotguns, in gauges 12, 16, and 20. We can't use buckshot. They have fully rifled barrels on most of them, and slugs designed for that barrel, so they can shoot a pretty tight pattern out to a hundred yards and more. They're almost as good as a black-powder rifle, which is also legal here, and a hunter can choose whether he wants to use black powder or a shotgun. In muzzleloaders, I like the new break-action versions, especially the Thompson Center Omega. Connecticut Valley Arms and Knight also have one. They break at the breech instead of being fixed, so they're easier to clean and care for. For anyone looking to buy one, I'd say get one of them.

Gary Drinkall: I like a .270 on up to a .300 Winchester Magnum because they shoot nice and flat. The bottom line is to get a good hole in the deer, and in this snow-covered country the shots are often long, and I like something flat and true.

Rene Semple: Anything in the .300 Winchester Magnum class. We don't have a lot of long shots, but they can present in odd ways so you don't get a perfect broadside. Also, they can tend to be back in the brush, and the .300 seems to be pretty good in that situation. For clients I recommend anything in the .30-caliber class or better.

Jim Shockey: While I personally hunt with a muzzleloader, we take 126 hunters per year, so I see 126 times as many people as myself hunting with conventional rifles. I'm a black-powder hunter, but you're darn right I have opinions on centerfire rifles. In my opinion, there's no such thing as overkill. If I had my way everybody would show up with a .338 Winchester Magnum or a .300 Weatherby Magnum, or something in the same category. That's what we tell our clients, or else they can bring something a little on either side of these.

We tell them to stay away from the 7mm magnum because in my opinion it's one of the most pathetic calibers ever invented. The bullets are too fast and they're too light, so you have problems with any kind of deflection, and problems with penetration. There are even too many deflections within the animal's body that cause inexcusable problems, like wounded animals. If a guy is really careful and uses a proper bullet with a 7mm, it will work just fine. If the guy is a tremendous shot it'll work just fine, too. But we've had far more wounded animals with the 7mm over the years than with any other caliber.

Duwane Adams: I'm a magnum man. I have the clients sight their rifles dead on at 300 yards. Then I have them shoot a target at 400 yards and mark on a piece of paper how many inches it dropped. Then I have them shoot it at 500 yards and write that down, too. I want that piece of paper taped on the stock of their rifles while we're hunting! And that's how we do it. I tell people the .300 Winchester Magnum is the rifle to bring.

Carlos Gonzalez Hermosillo: I personally prefer the .300 Winchester Magnum. It's a big gun, but I don't care about the kick. We sometimes must shoot at a long distance, and I like to feel confident that I can kill any animal a long distance off. It's a long-distance game at a small target, and you've got to have a rifle that's up to the task. In all my camps I have .264 Winchester Magnums, .270 Winchesters for the ladies and young people, or hunters who don't like the recoil, and also the 7mm Remington Magnums. If I'm asked what to bring, I tell them to bring the fastest, longest-shooting rifle they can shoot well.

Kirk Kelso: My favorite calibers are the "Big 7s" and the "Big 30s"—that is, the 7mm magnums and the .300 magnums. It doesn't necessarily take that kind of rifle to kill a Coues

How the hunter handles the rifle in the field is closely observed by whitetail guides, for obvious safety reasons.

whitetail, but it's sure a little more practical when you have to do the long-range game, which Coues deer hunting can certainly be at times. When you're shooting across canyons and dealing with the winds and longer distances, those flat-shooting "Big 7s" and "Big 30s" can sure be an advantage. For clients I'd recommend any rifle they can shoot the best. If a client is not comfortable with the magnums, I'd rather he bring a .243 that he shoots proficiently than a big gun that he can't shoot accurately.

What is your advice on bullet weight? Bullet construction?

Hal Blood: I like the 180-grain round-nosed bullets. I used to do handloads, and I like the Remington Core-Lokt bullets a lot.

Jeff Charles: I like the heavier bullets. As far as construction goes, I've always gone with Nosler Partition bullets. I've tried everything else, and in my opinion they're just unbeatable. I use them for moose, for deer, for everything. The problem with some of the others is that they're too hard, and you get a complete pass-through that doesn't do enough damage.

Dan Rosman: I've always been a fan of something in the 180-grain range. As far as construction goes, we see them all up here. It seems like the Nosler Partitions are pretty good in most rifles.

Chris Pevey: That's an area that can be the source of major dispute, but I'm a big ballistic tip fan. I like them because they do a lot of damage and the deer doesn't run far. You get good penetration and a good exit wound. I like a medium-weight bullet, but not a really heavy one. Whatever shoots well in the hunter's rifle is fine with me, but I prefer a medium-weight ballistic tip.

Charles Ruth: Again, keep in mind that we're in the Southeast, and I like to see a bullet weight that's appropriate for Southeastern game. In .30 caliber, I like no more than 150-grain bullets, because when you get up into the heavier loads you start to have a significantly heavier jacket that inhibits expansion. The shot punches a hole through the animal rather than expanding, which gets us to a discussion of bullet construction. I like to see highly expandable bullets, such as ballistic tips and bronze points, instead of controlled expansion bullets like the Barnes X, various partition types, or a Grand Slam.

My scientific statistics actually fell out significantly different on the performance of these two types of bullets. This means, in a nutshell, that when hunting our size of deer you want a lighter bullet that is designed to have enhanced bullet expansion. I think "Ballistic Tip" is Federal's brand name, but the term is used generally now for any bullet that uses a wedge principle, whereby something is driven down into the bullet from the tip in order to enhance expansion.

Jay Steen: I like the Ballistic Tip type of bullets, in the 130-grain for the .270 and 150-grain for the .30-06.

David Davis: Bullet weight would be what the gun was designed around, such as the 140-grain bullet in the 7mm magnum. The .300 Winchester Magnum was designed around a 180-grain bullet and the .338 was designed around a 250-grain bullet. In our region, I would stay at the medium-to-heavy end of the spectrum, in order to get deeper penetration and reduced brush deflection. My favorite bullet is the Swift Sirocco, and my least favorite is the Barnes X-Bullet. The Barnes X is a great bullet, but it will ruin a rifle barrel. Even with the coatings they use, these bullets can be problematic because over time the coating bonds with the casing and you get pressures that are astronomical. If you use these bullets with the "moly" coating, shoot them up within a year or so. All bullets misdirect some when they hit, but the Barnes X-Bullet is far worse to misdirect significantly because the center of gravity is still so far forward after the petals deploy. We've had some shots with Barnes X-Bullets that went in one side and came out the same side.

Mike Gardner: I'm an advocate of softpoints, like Remington's version. Nowadays there are so many different kinds of bullets and weights to choose from, but I've always had good experience with the Remington softpoints. They're just off-the-shelf factory ammo, but they do a good job.

Don White: I'm more worried about bullet placement than bullet construction. However, I would recommend at least 145-grain bullets. I'm not a big believer that bullet construction makes much difference, because there are so many good bullets out there now. I'd recommend whatever shoots best in your rifle.

Eric Albus: I'm a fan of heavy-caliber bullets, though it shouldn't be overdone. In the .270, use 150-grain bullets; in the .30-06, 165-grain bullets; in the .284 (7mm), 160-grain bullets; in the .300s, 180-grain bullets. There really isn't much need for the expensive premium bullets on the market today when you're hunting a thin-skinned animal like deer. The super bullets, as I call them, are really expensive, and they just do not expand enough in a deer. I have seen some dismal failures with such bullets in the last couple of years. The only need for a premium bullet is when you're shooting a light caliber, like a .243, because then penetration becomes an issue.

Keaton Kelso: I don't have a whole lot to say about bullet construction, because I don't have a favorite. I never recommend anything over 150-grain bullets. We had some guys last year who were shooting 250-grain bullets, but at longer distances

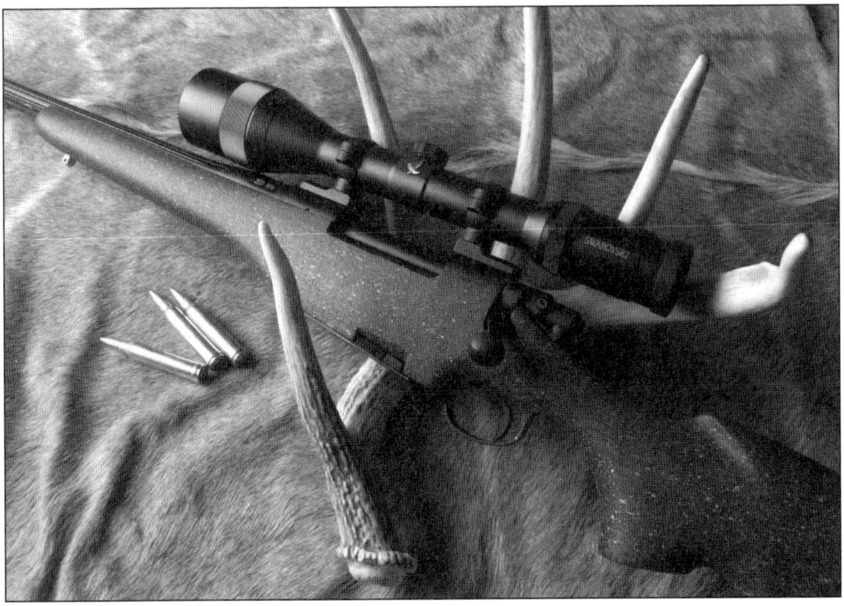

Hunting arms evoke a wide range of opinions among guides who hunt different situations and locations. (Photo courtesy of Bill Honza)

there's far too much drop with a bullet that heavy. The 150-grain bullet will kill any whitetail in North America, and it shoots flat, too.

James Woodley: I don't have much of an opinion on this one, since we do mostly bow hunts. I do like the Powerbelt slugs in shotguns, as well as the Barnes Expanders. As far as broadheads go, I'd recommend a fixed-blade broadhead as opposed to a mechanical one, but I don't think it's a big deal. The speeds and penetration they're getting with today's arrows are phenomenal. I've done some research on the deer we've harvested versus those we've wounded and lost, and I haven't really seen a big difference between the two kinds of broadheads. Some of the outfitters have outlawed mechanical broadheads, but we haven't, primarily because we can't demonstrate a clear advantage of one over the other. It really goes back to shot placement more than the type or weight of broadhead, I think. Nevertheless, I'd still recommend the fixed-blade over the mechanical.

Gary Drinkall: In the .270, which is my personal favorite, I like a 130-grain bullet because it shoots nice and flat and it hits hard enough to do the job. As to the type of bullet, I like Nosler Partition bullets.

Rene Semple: From 165 grains up to 180 grains. I'd tend to weight them toward the heavier side because of the brush in our area and the fact that some of our animals are really big. A mature white-tailed buck in this region can go up to 350 pounds. As far as bullet construction goes, I'm not particular, but the Nosler Partition and the Trophy Bonded Bear Claw are both good. As long as it's a good controlled-expansion bullet, it should do the job.

Jim Shockey: I like a heavier bullet. I'm not a fan, as I said earlier, of light, fast bullets. In the .300 Weatherby, I'd suggest a 200-grain bullet. As for bullet construction, I think one of the best bullets out there right now is the Nosler Partition Gold. The Trophy Bonded is good, as is the Swift A-frame, and the Barnes X-Bullets will work, too.

Duwane Adams: As for bullet construction, I'm a very big fan of the Hornady bullets. I think they're very innovative in what they're doing, and I think they're ahead of the curve as compared to most bullet manufacturers. They've come out with some innovative products. The weight of the bullet is not as important, and I'll tell you why. If the rifle is shooting dead on at 300 yards, and we know the exact drop at 400 and 500 yards, we can make the shot with any weight of bullet. I personally shoot a 150-grain bullet, and it's very adequate for Coues deer.

Carlos Gonzalez Hermosillo: I like medium bullet weights for the caliber being used. I don't like the very light ones, and I don't like the very heavy ones. In the .300, I like 180-grain bullets, in the .264 the 140-grain bullet, in the .270 the 130-grain bullet, and in the 7mm the 160-grain bullet. I like to be able to shoot long distances, and also shoot through brush the first hundred yards, and the medium bullet weights are the best combination. For brands, I like the Nosler Partition, the Swift, the Ballistic Tips, and the ones with plastic tips so they don't disintegrate on impact.

Kirk Kelso: These are not big concerns on the Coues whitetails because they're small animals and it doesn't take a lot to get the job done. If the bullet shoots well in the gun, that's the best bullet as far as I'm concerned.

Do you have any tips on shooting techniques in field situations?

Hal Blood: We have to shoot quickly a lot of the time. Too many people think they're going to get a standing, broadside shot, but I don't often get one of those. If a guy's not comfortable taking a running shot, I don't make him take it. I do tell people it's good to practice this kind of shot, because it may be your best chance to take a deer. They can practice by putting a cardboard target in a tire and having someone roll it down a hill for them, letting it bounce, and then shooting at the moving target. I think the best practice for shooting running deer is rabbit hunting, and shooting at running rabbits. They kind of jump and run in the same way as deer, and if you can get proficient at shooting running rabbits you can kill a running deer.

The biggest tip is to be ready to pull the trigger as soon as the cross hairs settle where you want them. You don't wait, because your rifle is just an extension of your arm, and you do it all in one motion and very quickly.

Jeff Charles: My best tip is to get a rest, especially if you get the drop on the deer by seeing him first. So often the hunter sees the deer, and he aims at it with the rifle barrel waving around, and he misses. Right next to him stands a sapling he could easily have used for a rest, and his chances would have gone up tremendously.

Dan Rosman: More and more clients are bringing shooting sticks. At first I thought it was a real hassle to carry the things, but you can get off much better shots using them. Up here there aren't many times you can lie on your belly and take a shot.

Chris Pevey: Take a good rest and make a confident shot. Those "Hail Mary" shots don't cut it. If it crosses your mind that it might be a bad shot, it's probably going to be a bad shot, so don't take it. Wait for the right shot, and a good broadside presentation is best.

Charles Ruth: By all means, do everything you can to use a solid rest. When I was actively guiding, we used large stands with excellent rests, and that was one key to our repeated success. The average person can't do very well offhand at a distance of more than fifty yards or so. Try not to put yourself in a position where you're going to have to shoot freehand, because the results are demonstrably poorer when you do. Use a rest.

Jay Steen: We've got everybody hunting from stands, and we have too many hunters who will rest their barrel on the armrest, instead of resting the forearm grip on it. That can surely make your gun shoot funny. Get a good, firm rest, but be sure the barrel isn't resting on something that could throw the shot off.

David Davis: A shooting stick is a great thing to have when hunting whitetails in our region. The ground cover won't let you use a bipod very often, because you're sitting down in it. But the shooting sticks work great. Also, use the lowest scope power, and never crank it up to the highest power. We also have every hunter shoot at the range before we go into the field, because

Rifle hunting is by far the most popular form of whitetail hunting. (Photo courtesy of Keaton Kelso)

we want to make sure the gun is on target, and we also want to observe how the hunter handles the firearm.

Mike Gardner: The single most important thing I look for when we get ready to harvest a buck is to get the client to really relax, take his time, and squeeze in a very controlled fashion. We see a lot of folks who put the cross hairs on the animal and just jerk that trigger. Well, when you pull the trigger that way, the gun moves before the bullet comes out of the barrel. If you watch really, really good shooters, they relax and take their time, take a breath before they squeeze, and then squeeze that trigger so lightly that when the gun goes off it surprises them. The animal's there; he's not going anywhere. Don't look at the rack, but just try to focus right on the point of contact where you want to place that bullet. I really encourage a client to wait until the deer is broadside and then aim for the broad part of the shoulder. If you move a little, and you're off a couple of inches, you're still going to be OK because it's a big target.

Don White: Our ranch has very, very thick brush, and it's really difficult hunting. I always recommend that the client put the shot on the point of the shoulder so that he hits the animal in the bone and drops it. Long shots are great, but 50 yards is like 10 miles down there while you're tracking. We stay away from chest shots because their chests are so tough from the terrain of their habitat. Going through the tough brush where they live, they've built up a plate there that's hard to penetrate. As for handling the firearm, always use a steady rest. We mostly hunt out of tripods, and your right elbow and right hand are the most important parts anatomically. Always get a steady rest, even if it's a 30-yard shot.

Eric Albus: Take a good rest before shooting. Find something, a rock, a daypack, a tree stump, or anything else that will steady those cross hairs.

Keaton Kelso: If there's a buck in the brush, try to get a hole through the brush so you can kill it. A really big whitetail isn't going to expose itself in an open alfalfa patch until it's just about dark. If you can see him, though, you can often find a pie-plate-size opening in the brush so you can sling a bullet in there and kill that buck. If you're shooting a pretty big caliber, such as the .300 magnum, you'd have to hit a pretty big stick to knock the bullet off enough to miss. I also tell guys to carry shooting sticks with them. They'll have a deer out there at 300 yards and they'll try to freehand it. It's impossible, so shooting sticks in the field are on our equipment list.

We also have all our hunters shoot at the range after they get here, but then I have them lean up against a tree and try it. There are a lot of guys who can put round after round in the bull's-eye from sandbags, but when you put them in a different situation they fall completely apart. We find that out when they rest on a tree.

James Woodley: You've got to be able to judge your distance, especially when you're bowhunting like we usually do. That's a big factor for us because a lot of our hunters come from back

East and they're used to deer with smaller body sizes than ours. We hunt on open field edges, and when you get a big deer out in the open, he looks like he's a lot closer than he actually is. Since we are bowhunting, one of my biggest recommendations is to bring a rangefinder and be able to get the distance exactly.

Gary Drinkall: Most of my scenarios involve shooting out of blinds and stands, so the shooting position is sitting down. One thing I'd note is that some guys have run into deer on their way in to the stand and haven't taken a shot because they figure they're going to see the buck again. I tell them no, get some lead in the air, because generally when it's a really big deer, a book deer, you're not going to see him more than once. So as far as shooting techniques go, a hunter should definitely practice shooting offhand before he goes on a hunt.

Another problem with my baits and my stands is that the hunter gets so excited when a big buck finally steps out that he can't make long shots. I pretty well have to keep all my food plots within 200 yards of the stand or there's no way he can make the shot. I had a guy last year who had a monster buck come out on a food plot at 1:00 P.M., and he got so excited that he blew the job! He watched the deer for ten minutes, and he knew it was a monster. He had plenty of time, but he just couldn't make the shot.

Rene Semple: If you can get a rest, always do so, rather than shooting freehand. A good, solid rest will always enhance your shot placement.

Jim Shockey: This is obvious, but whenever possible take a rest. Don't push beyond your own abilities. Any shot that risks wounding an animal is a shot that shouldn't be taken. There's enough of a measure of risk just by pulling the trigger while aiming at an animal, let alone purposely taking a chance beyond your own abilities. If you're just going to be shooting and hoping, don't take the shot.

Duwane Adams: Keep in mind that we do a lot of really long-range shooting. The biggest thing the hunter needs to do, after he has down exactly where the bullet is hitting at various distances, is to go back to the rifle range. Most people don't do that. You need to learn to shoot off a backpack and in various different positions and situations. That's what I tell clients, that if they think there's going to be a bench rest out there, they're on drugs! The animal isn't going to see us, but you've got to get prepared for those situations.

In my opinion, a bipod is a great help for distances under about three hundred yards, but if you're going to use one for farther than that you've got to get a rest for the butt, or else it's still going up and down and you're going to miss. I like to have the guy lie down and have the rifle dead solid. If you use a bipod for long shots, you've got to get something under the butt of the rifle to stabilize it, too, or the rifle will definitely be bobbing up and down. And remember, the chest cavity of a Coues deer is about twelve inches from the top of his back to the bottom of his chest. There's just no room for a big error, and you've got to drop it right in there.

Carlos Gonzalez Hermosillo: I always have my hunters find a rest. I don't let them shoot offhand. On a Coues deer hunt we're shooting long-range, and on a quality guided hunt the

Is your rifle capable, and are you proficient enough, to reach out and take this great buck? (Photo courtesy of Don White)

hunter is shooting a very expensive bullet! You've got to get a good rest!

Kirk Kelso: The hunters have to practice in shooting positions other than from the bench, because that's how to become proficient in the field. They need to practice shooting from the kneeling position, prone, and any other situation they might encounter while actually hunting. Remember, you're not going to be carrying a bench in the field, so odd situations need to be practiced ahead of time.

How do you prepare for and handle "buck fever" (overpowering excitement) in a hunter/client?

Hal Blood: Because of the way I hunt, there really isn't time for it to develop. Everything happens quickly. Buck fever generally comes if you're sitting and waiting, and you see one coming. It takes a while to get within range, and then it takes some more time to present a good shot, and the nerves start to work on you. I've really never run into that in any of my hunters because there's always somebody with them and also things happen so quickly. Most of the time I say, "There he is, take him," and it's over suddenly.

Jeff Charles: I've thought over and over about that question, and you just can't prevent "buck fever" in clients. There's absolutely no way! You can try to prepare them for what to expect and go over it with them in advance, but when it comes to actually squeezing the trigger, they're on their own. Experience is the best cure for it, in my opinion. After you shoot a few deer and get some hunting under your belt, you still feel the thrill of the hunt, but you're more in control of your emotions.

Dan Rosman: My approach is to talk calmly and quietly to them and try not to let them look too long at any animal through the riflescope. If I see they're starting to get a little too excited, I tell them to put the rifle down and not look at the deer. When they've calmed down, I tell them that when they pick that thing up, just look at the deer's body, don't look at the head, don't look at the antlers, and don't look at anything except where they're going to shoot. I nestle right up against them, and I'm careful how I talk to them, because that can sometimes get them over the edge. I just try to talk them gently through it. I had one guy I'll never forget who was a professional weightlifter, a real monster of a man. He saw this deer, and it wasn't even that big a deer, and he started hyperventilating and coming unglued. I had to set his rifle down and talk to him, and luckily the deer hung around long enough for me to get him settled down, and he did kill it. But that was the worst case of buck fever I've ever seen.

Chris Pevey: I still get it myself, and when I quit getting it, I'm going to quit hunting! I like the way the question is worded—"overpowering excitement"—because that's exactly what it is. I really enjoy seeing a client get excited, but it can be too much. I take a lot of kids hunting, and what I do with them is try to get them to settle down and get a good, steady trigger pull. Most of the time I'm on the stand with the client, because we have a 115-point minimum here at Millhaven, and most guys just don't know how to judge bucks. Since I'm right there, I can talk them through it. I can't just put them on the stand and tell them to shoot the best buck they see, because they'll kill my best two-and-a-half-year-old bucks. I tell them that I'll let them know when to take the safety off, not to put their finger near the trigger until I say so, and so on. But I do like to see them get excited, because it allows me to live the thrill through someone else's excitement.

Charles Ruth: That's really tough, but being intimately familiar with the firearm is one key to controlling buck fever. You certainly don't want issues of muzzle blast, recoil, flinching, all these factors, coming into play, because that's just going to compound the problem. So right at the top of my list of preventive measures is familiarity with and confidence in your weapon. That removes at least one controllable factor from the equation. Beyond that, it's hard to get into somebody's mind, and that's where the problem is with buck fever. It's all a mind game, just like golf.

Jay Steen: When they see something in the woods that turns out to be a shooter, you just have to have them prepared

Muzzleloader expert and guide Jim Shockey stresses the importance of practice with your chosen weapon, be it centerfire rifle, muzzleloader, or bow. (Photo courtesy of Jim Shockey)

to forget the antlers and concentrate on picking out a spot on the deer to shoot. They should try to consider it just another deer. Since we're usually not in the stand with them, the personal things you can do to calm people down all have to be done ahead of time.

David Davis: I make them turn around and not look at the deer. If I see my hunter coming unraveled, I just tell him to turn around and look at me. Then I tell him to his face, "It's just a deer, that's all it is. Now turn around and kill it." And he will, almost every time.

Mike Gardner: I just sit there and tell them to relax, because the deer's not going anywhere. I tell them to take their time and do a good squeeze of the trigger. And I assure them that if by chance the deer walks off, we've got plenty of time to find another one.

Don White: There was one story I'd heard for years, and I didn't think it was true until I saw it happen. The hunter had a

.308 lever-action, and he ejected all his rounds without pulling the trigger! He was so excited that he thought he was shooting, and he asked, "Where am I hitting?" I told him, "You're not shooting!" He looked down and there were five rounds on the ground! That was interesting. To overcome buck fever, I have the hunter stop, use good breath control, and get a good rest. I'm locked in with my binoculars, so I'm trying to get an idea of where the shots are hitting, and it sure helps to get them calmed down so I'm not distracted.

Eric Albus: First and foremost, we won't let such a response in the hunter compromise anyone's safety. Excitement in a guy with a firearm can certainly lead to a dangerous situation. A lot of times we'll try to talk the guy through the shot, if we're sitting with him. Usually that helps. We've found that with most guys, buck fever is not really an overwhelming issue.

Keaton Kelso: Typically, I'm constantly talking to the hunters. I tell them to hold steady, squeeze the trigger slowly, take a deep breath first, and so on. I try to get their minds off the animal and onto the shot as much as possible. If I tell them it's a good buck, I don't even want them to look at the antlers, because as soon as they do, that's when they lose everything. I tell them to concentrate on the body and on placing the shot well, and I'm constantly talking them through the process. We can look at the antlers later at our leisure if they make a good shot. I've been in situations where the client is so excited he can't find the buck in his scope, so I get behind him and he's about two hundred yards off from where he ought to be looking. From there you just have to talk him through the process gradually and hope that it's a situation where you have time to straighten him out.

James Woodley: I don't really know how to answer that, because we're not on the stand with our clients. We make it clear to our hunters that for a deer to be a shooter it has to be wider than the ears and at least eight points. We're looking for a minimum of 130 B&C points. Basically, I tell guys that if you see one and you're getting all nervous, it's probably a shooter. If you've got to sit there and wonder whether it's big enough or not, it's probably not as big as you think it might be. As for dealing with excitement and getting a shot off, I don't have much to offer in the way of tips on that. It's pretty much up to the hunter to control it when the situation comes along. Now, after the shot when you're bowhunting, you've also got to deal with the excitement factor. Some guys can get the shot off, and then after they make a hit, they just quit thinking and go right after the deer. They've got to wait and give the deer time to expire, or they can push him out of the county.

Gary Drinkall: Boy, I wish somebody could tell me. You just have to slow the hunters down by preparing them ahead of time as best you can, especially when it's a stand scenario and you're not physically present with them. If I'm with them, I use gentle talking, staying calm myself, telling them to gently squeeze the trigger. But guys get so excited about a really big buck that they can miss the chance of a lifetime. I try to talk them through it so that doesn't happen.

Rene Semple: That's pretty tough, but the best method is to stay calm yourself. We get excited ourselves when we see a really big buck, but we can't let it show! The guide has to stay calm, because if he doesn't, the client won't be far behind in getting excited.

Jim Shockey: I handle it two ways: If "buck fever" is completely lacking, I might just add a little of it. If it's there in overabundance, I'll calm the client down. The easiest way is to take his mind off the hunt, make a sideways joke that takes his attention off what's right in front of him—something totally absurd like "Hey, your shoelace is undone!" This changes the client's thought pattern away from the welling panic inside him. At that point, your voice is everything. If you in any way sound excited and enthusiastically voice that excitement, then you will surely transfer that feeling to the client. That's especially true if the hunter has a leaning in that direction anyway.

Duwane Adams: It happens every year. The experience that we have of consistently finding bucks makes all the difference. I have a lot of clients who shoot and miss. The best thing you can do when they miss is to tell them it doesn't matter because you're going to find them another buck. And if they absolutely believe that you're going to do that, they'll follow you to hell and back. I make it clear that I'm never going to give up on them; I don't care how many times they fall apart. I repeatedly tell them that if they miss again, I'm going to find them another buck. And I've found that this approach cures buck fever in a lot of cases. I tell these guys that I'm not their guide, I'm their best friend, and if they'll do what I say in every situation, they're going to kill a buck.

Carlos Gonzalez Hermosillo: Everybody's different, and you have to handle them as individuals. You just have to be ready for anything that happens. I've seen people shooting inch-and-

Guide Duwane Adams's hunters regularly kill Coues bucks at 400-plus yards. Is your rifle capable of such a shot? (Photo courtesy of Duwane Adams)

a-half groups at 200 yards, bullet after bullet. One of these people was a sheep hunter, and he'd paid a huge sum of money to hunt the sheep. My part was to get him within about two hundred yards of the animal one time, and when we do this, my obligation is met. The first time this guy shot twice at a sheep at 127 yards, and he missed both times! I let him keep hunting, and the second time he shot was at 157 yards, and he missed three times. Then he missed two times at 175 yards. He asked, "Carlos, can we go on shooting?" I had to tell him, "No, my friend. We've been 15 days in the field, and you've had three opportunities, two more than I guaranteed. I think that this time the sheep walks."

People just get excited, and I don't know how to cure it. I had one lady hunter who could see the deer, and she raised up the rifle and swore she shot. She asked me if she hit the animal, and she hadn't pulled the trigger! She swore she was shooting, and I told her that she wasn't shooting and that she should pull the trigger, but she wouldn't pull the trigger. She was convinced she was shooting!

I had another hunter who did exactly the same thing as the lady hunter. I had yet another hunter who was supposed to be a really good shot, and he passed up many excellent deer looking for Mr. Big. Finally, there was Mr. Big about a hundred and fifty yards away, lying under a bush. He was a little bit behind the brush, but it was a perfect shot for anybody, and this guy was a good shot. He missed a couple of yards to the right, then a couple of yards under; then the deer got up and he shot a couple of yards over it. He got so mad he threw the rifle down and broke it into two pieces! How can I react to that? I just don't ever get angry with them. I just tell them it's their party, and they're paying for it. It's an excitement that many people can't control, and I don't know what to do about it.

Kirk Kelso: I don't think there's any way you can effectively prepare for it. Even as a guide, you're not going to expect it to happen. When the deer's there, everything's kind of in a hurry, and it's impossible for the guide to anticipate exactly what the client might do. The guide is concentrating on the animal to see where the shot's going to go, so he might not be able to watch for early signs of a problem. We're usually in a situation of a fairly long shot, and the deer doesn't know we're there. If I see a client getting shaken up, I make him stop, start over completely, and get his breathing under control; I try to get him calmed down. I've kind of developed a little program so that when a guy's lying prone, resting on a pack or something, and he's shaking and hyperventilating, I reach over and put my hand in the middle of his back, and often just that little touch from me, just knowing I'm there, will calm him right down.

Do you have any wise words on bowhunting? Black-powder hunting?

Hal Blood: I take a few bow hunters, but you can bet it's tougher up here. I tell bow hunters they're going to have to be more patient than they are most places, because deer densities aren't what they are in other places. Bow hunters here are going to be in a blind or a tree stand. We do quite a lot of muzzleloader hunts, and there's really not much difference between hunting with a rifle and a muzzleloader anymore, especially with the new in-line types. Our muzzleloader season is late, after the regular season, so it's going to be cold. I always tell the hunters to prepare for foul weather, and make sure their muzzleloader is moistureproof. Damp snow that melts on your gun and then freezes is worse than anything else. Typically we don't have many exceptionally long shots here, unless a guy is hunting around a clear-cut or something, so a muzzleloader works just fine. The farthest deer I ever shot was about a hundred and twenty yards away, but most of our shots are about fifty yards.

Jeff Charles: Yes, we do both, and it's extremely important to prepare the hunter for a one-shot hunt. I also prepare my rifle hunters the same way, because even then it's the first shot that counts. With a bow or a black-powder rifle, it's obviously a one-shot deal almost certainly. For the bow hunter, once the deer is inside twenty-five yards, you've got the upper hand at

Short-action rifles without scopes and slug guns are often preferable in Maine's big woods because shots are often quick and close. (Photo courtesy of Hal Blood)

that point. The hunter needs to wait for the perfect shot, when the deer puts its head down or looks the other way. Today's muzzleloaders are so accurate at 100 yards, but you've only got that one shot, so make it good. Also, we owe it to the animal to make a humane, clean kill, and a one-shot kill is the way to go.

Dan Rosman: I don't have any major insights into either. I've had more bad luck with bowhunting than I want to think about. If I'm going to take a bow hunter, I want him to be almost a professional bow hunter, somebody who's really serious about it. We get a lot of guys up north here who just do it to try to extend their season, and they're not very good at it, and they wind up frustrated, and that's frustrating to me. Black powder now just requires that you practice, but otherwise it's not much different from regular rifle hunting.

Chris Pevey: Practice is the best advice I can give. Know the ability of your equipment, and know what you can do with your equipment. Then you've got to practice to be proficient. I'm a full-time bow hunter now, and I have to practice every day. Additionally, use good equipment! I had a guy show up one day who didn't have an arrow or a broadhead that matched. We took him to the local archery shop and got him shooting decently. As for black powder, most guys pick up a black-powder gun, shoot it a couple of times, and then go out hunting. They need to really familiarize themselves with the weapon. The same goes for crossbows. Is the client a twenty-yard man, a thirty-yard man, or what, with a bow? Can he consistently make a thirty-yard shot? The same goes for black powder. Hunters need to know their personal effective range, and the weapon is usually a lot better than the shooter.

Charles Ruth: I've done some guiding of bow hunters, though we get about 90 percent rifle hunters. As for most of the black-powder rifles that are out there today, I'd say there isn't much difference between them and modern centerfire rifles. For archery hunting, there's a lot more preparation involved, and the wind is even more important than it is with rifle hunting. Ideally, you're trying to get the hunter within some twenty yards of the deer, and the wind is the number one factor. If you can't beat the deer's nose, you're not going to be successful. For a guide, that's the ultimate challenge, having everything laid out and well planned, and then selecting the proper hunting area for the day based on the wind. In all hunting situations, in order to have the best possibilities of success you've got to go as often as you can, keep an open mind, and be flexible.

Jay Steen: We don't do much black-powder hunting. We've got a five-day black-powder season just before the regular gun season, but we don't take hunters then because a lot of our regular clients expect to be the first gun hunters in the woods here. All the black-powder hunters we've had come during regular rifle season. In bowhunting, with the newer bows and sights, people have a tendency to try to shoot deer at a range that's farther than their equipment and personal capabilities can handle. If you're shooting 3-D targets, they don't move, and people tend to think that because they can hit a 3-D target consistently at a certain distance, they ought to be able to hit a deer every time at that distance, but it's a lot different in a hunting situation. The bow hunter should be very aware of the capability of his equipment and what he personally is capable of doing when actually hunting.

David Davis: The key to bowhunting is to watch the wind. If you can get downwind, you're in business. I used to be a dedicated bow hunter, but I've given it up for lack of time to practice. I just got into black powder again recently, using an old .45-70 Sharps. I'm not really familiar enough with the latest black-powder technology to comment in detail, but some of the new scoped in-line guns are capable of 250-yard shots, making five-inch groups, so there's essentially no difference in hunting technique with them. Today's designs can no longer be called primitive weapons.

You're going to have to be much closer with the bow, so you should get as far away as you can and watch where the deer are moving in and out of cover. I don't necessarily like the word "pattern," because it's hard to pattern a Texas deer like you might where there are 10,000 acres of wheat and 100 acres of creek bottom. You can pattern a deer there, but not here. But

Bow hunters must be particularly practiced and cool when a monster like this shows up under their stand. (Photo courtesy of James Woodley)

if you simply figure out where they're moving most frequently, you can plan your setup better.

Mike Gardner: We don't take either kind of hunter, so I don't have much information to offer. It's not that I don't support those types of hunting, but right now we're just not set up for them in terms of how our stands are arranged.

Don White: My advice is to save those things until you have a solid understanding of whitetail behavior and you've developed good tracking skills. You're going to have to do some tracking when you use those weapons. However, black powder is getting really good, but with all the smoke generated you may not see exactly where the animal goes after the shot. With a bow you'll have to track every time. Get a few years of hunting under your belt before you try either of these weapons, so you're already a proficient hunter.

Eric Albus: Bowhunting is what we're probably most famous for here at Milk River Outfitters. Being mentally prepared for the shot is so very, very important. If the hunter would just visualize the shot before he's even in the field, and be mentally prepared to make that shot, the kill rate would skyrocket. Lack of mental preparation is the biggest obstacle to effective bowhunting. Unfortunately, we have a lot of guys that come in and get rattled, and miss shots at fifteen yards, shots they would make time after time on a target. That's simply a sign of the missing ingredient, mental preparation. As for black-powder hunting, I don't have a lot of experience with it. We've had several guys take deer with the new in-line muzzleloaders, and if I were going to black-powder hunt, that's what I'd use.

Keaton Kelso: Scent control is the number one thing. With black powder in Kansas you can't use scopes, so it's a fifty-yard game, no matter how you cut it, either bow or black powder. That time of year, if you spot a good buck, you've got an excellent chance of killing him if you get right down in the brush with him, and if you control your scent adequately. The other thing is practice. You must practice more than you would with your rifle. That's especially true with the bow. If you're not practicing once a week during the off-season, you're just not doing what it takes to kill a good buck at forty yards.

James Woodley: Practice so you know where it's hitting at different distances. It's foolish not to do that in any case, but especially if you're paying for a hunt. We've had guys come on a hunt in the past, and they only shoot their bows a day before they leave to come here. It's frustrating on both ends when they do that. I mentioned earlier the new break-action muzzleloaders, and they also have a new powder that's been out a couple of years, called Triple-7, and it burns a lot cleaner. You just drop two or three pellets down the barrel, then your slug, and you're ready to go.

Gary Drinkall: I have very little experience with either.

Rene Semple: I am a bow hunter, and it's all I do now for myself. For bowhunting, it's pretty straightforward—patience and practice. We don't do any black-powder hunts.

Jim Shockey: You can't be too careful on your shot selection. I continually see bow hunters winging an arrow in the direction of the animal, and the shot is far beyond their abilities. They need to wait, wait, wait for the deer to move closer. If you choose to bowhunt, then do it ethically, and that means knowing both your equipment and your abilities, and waiting for the right shot and situation.

For black-powder hunting, it's the same thing. Remember, you've decided to hunt with a weapon that is inferior to a high-powered rifle in its capabilities, so get closer! Don't simply shoot and hope. Don't shoot beyond any distance at which you're absolutely confident you can make a great shot. With either bow or black powder, you're hunting with a primitive weapon, and as good as you might be, there's inherently more possibility of something going awry. Don't push the capabilities of the weapon by exceeding the distance that those weapons are designed to shoot.

Duwane Adams: The biggest problem with both these weapons is that most people who use them try to stalk these deer. Dwight Schuh, editor of *Bowhunting* magazine, is a good friend of mine, and he's hunted with me three times. He and Wayne Carlton and Larry Jones, all well-known bow hunters, have hunted with me. So far, none of them has killed a Coues deer with a bow! And these are some of the world's best bow hunters, OK? Coues are the most difficult deer in the whole world to stalk and kill with a bow. In my opinion, you've got to quit trying. The best way to kill a Coues deer with a bow is to hunt over water, and you have to hunt early, in September, when they come to drink quite a bit.

As for black powder, the new black-powder rifles they have today are just devastating, and they've got some great hunts for black-powder hunters only, here in Arizona. Half of them are unsubscribed—that is, not enough people apply to utilize the available tags. You just use the same hunting technique I described above, glassing and then stalking to within black-powder distance to shoot the deer. With today's modern black-powder rifles, you can consistently make shots of 150 to 200 yards, and you can get that close sometimes. Even if you blow three or four stalks, you usually will get your chance at some point.

Carlos Gonzalez Hermosillo: We have some hunters who use both. Coues deer hunting is a unique hunt, and where they live is extremely tough terrain for a bow hunter. You have to be either very, very lucky or very, very skillful to get within range with a bow and arrow. I have had bow hunters take animals, and I've had some miss animals. Luckily, nobody has wounded an animal we didn't recover, so we've avoided one thing I really hate. Hunting Coues deer with bow and arrow is an excellent, challenging sport, but I don't really think the killing power of an arrow is the best way to hunt these deer. I had one archer—and you and I know him very well—who could hit a Styrofoam water cup at 75 yards, but when his opportunity came, he missed.

With black powder, using the newer in-line muzzleloaders you should kill anything you shoot at within 200 yards or so. With a flintlock, of course, it's another story. Every time you shoot, your face is black from all the powder that comes out, and I couldn't hit a 55-gallon drum at 50 yards using one of those antiques!

Kirk Kelso: I want both types of hunters to be prepared for disappointment. Coues deer hunting is a tough game even with a high-powered rifle, let alone trying to get into close range so you can take them with a bow or a muzzleloader. It also can be a very boring type of hunting with a bow, because the hunter is often sitting over a water hole in the heat of the day, and it might not be the most enjoyable experience he's had.

Chapter 5

HUNTING WHITETAILS WITH THE GUIDES

What constitutes a successful hunt, from your perspective?

Hal Blood: A hunt is successful if the guide has put in a good effort, we've seen some deer, and had some close encounters. Up here it's not whether you get one or not. As long as the hunter's had a good time, learned some stuff, and so on, to me he's had a successful hunt. I don't have any hunters who don't see a deer, but some weeks it can be a struggle due to adverse weather conditions.

Jeff Charles: To me, it's when somebody says to me when it's over, "I've had a great time and I want to come back next year." You can't always measure a successful hunt by the game taken. Because it's big country we hunt, and because of the type of terrain we have, most hunters realize that they're not going to get a big deer every year. However, within a couple of years they will get a good deer if they persist. Our good hunters have just as much fun in the years they don't shoot a deer as they do in the years when they get one. You're trying to make memories that will last a lifetime, and when you do, that's success.

Dan Rosman: If I can show my client game, and he knows that I gave him 100 percent effort, it's a success. It's not always the kill that makes for success. When that hunter leaves, I want him to feel that I gave it everything I've got, even if for some reason things didn't go right and we didn't kill anything. So a happy client is a good measure of a successful hunt.

Chris Pevey: A hunt is successful if the hunter harvested a decent buck, but it's also successful if the guide was knowledgeable and possessed the necessary skills, and if the hunter had a good time, enjoyed the land, was treated well, and got to see a lot of interesting things. A good hunt is when the client walks away feeling like he got his money's worth.

Charles Ruth: Number one in my book is demonstrating to the hunter that you're prepared when he arrives in camp. Second, you've got to demonstrate to the hunter that you're working hard, and when the hunt is over the hunter knows you've given your all for him. It's not about harvesting game. It's about making your client understand that you did everything you could to make him successful. There are so many factors you can't control—weather, two or three days of hunting when the deer aren't moving, and so on. Most hunters understand that these are factors beyond the guide's control, so you've just got to show them you're doing all you can under the circumstances. A successful hunt would be when both you and the hunter know that you've done your best and everybody feels good about the effort.

Jay Steen: Naturally, getting a deer makes a hunt technically successful. The hunter has to enjoy the whole experience, though, from the lodging, meeting new people and getting to know them, learning something new, and so on, and it all goes into making a successful hunt. If you come and take an animal but have a poor experience in the camp, it's harder to feel good about the hunt.

David Davis: It's not all about the kill, but it's seeing the kind of buck you expected to see, whether you passed him up or shot him. It's seeing good deer activity, fights, chases, and the like. You don't have to kill a deer to have a good hunt. Sometimes guys make a big mistake passing a great buck early in the hunt, holding out for Mr. Wonderful. But they had a chance at a great buck and chose to pass, and they go home feeling successful. It's seeing mature bucks that fit into your expectations, whether you make the kill or not.

Mike Gardner: I really like it when both hunter and guide feel like they've hunted hard, spent the time needed, and had a good time doing it. I like it when we can sit back at the end of a hunt and say we saw a lot of game, and a lot of interesting things other than the game we were after. I like to see activity going on around us that the client probably has never seen before, and pay attention to small things by pointing them out, because that's part of the whole experience. I like it at the end of the hunt when we've built a friendship and we've had good fellowship. Many times when this is the case, at the end of the hunt we've also been rewarded with a really great animal.

Don White: To me it's seeing plenty of game and spending a lot of time in the field with good friends or making new friends while you're there. You don't necessarily have to take a deer to have a successful hunt.

Eric Albus: Success is defined in different ways for different people. For me, it has a lot to do with the camp atmosphere, the people I'm with, the game we take, and so on. As an outfitter, I often have to sit down and figure out what each client expects out of a hunt, and we work it out from there. You've got to make it an individual thing, by figuring out the needs of each client and trying to meet those needs. From my perspective, the ultimate in a successful hunt is a satisfied client who books again.

Keaton Kelso: A successful hunt is being on good property and seeing quality animals, and having a good, fun hunt where you enjoy yourself. I don't think the kill has anything to do with a successful whitetail hunt. That may be a different story for some very expensive hunts, like for bighorn sheep. But for whitetails, seeing good bucks and passing them because they aren't quite what you're looking for, that's a successful hunt, even if you never see the one you want. Having a good time and seeing game are tops in my book.

James Woodley: I'd count it successful if you get to see some deer, and hopefully a trophy buck, while you're hunting. For some guys, it takes a long time to kill a deer with a bow. We had a guy kill his first deer last year after ten trips here, so obviously he had some sense of success all those times he didn't get a deer. He'd seen some animals, but I think more than anything he just wanted to come back because he enjoyed the place and enjoyed the company and so on. That can be a successful hunt for many people.

Hunter and guide must work as a team to bring the hunt to a successful conclusion. (Photo courtesy of Bill Honza)

Gary Drinkall: Bagging your game, I guess, is the ultimate in success. I also count it successful if I can show the hunter lots of deer, even young bucks. You can't show all hunters a huge deer every day, but if you can show them lots of deer and lots of young bucks, to me that's successful even if that big dude doesn't step out. I've put that food plot out there and done my best, and if the big guy doesn't show up, that's not really my fault, especially if you've watched thirty to forty does in front of your stand and you've seen eight or ten bucks come by. To me, if my people are seeing lots of deer and lots of bucks, even if we don't shoot a 170-point deer every day, that's success.

Rene Semple: I'd have to say it's when a hunter doesn't get his game, but leaves happy and re-books. The most common measure of a successful hunt is to harvest an animal, and that doesn't always happen. If the guy doesn't take anything and leaves happy with the experience anyway, that's the epitome of success, in my book.

Jim Shockey: For me, a successful hunt is when the client walks away thinking he's just had the best hunt he could have possibly had, and has no complaints. That goes down even to the little things, like he wants hot water in his thermos instead of coffee. If I can get to the point where service-wise we've taken care of the client's every need, and we've fulfilled his expectations for the hunt, including the quality of animal he takes, and the quality of the experience, the guide, and the equipment, then I'd call that a successful hunt.

Duwane Adams: A successful hunt is in the eyes of the hunter, not in the eyes of the guide. When a person comes to hunt with me, I ask him several questions: What do you want to do? Is there anything you'd like to see, besides the hunting, since you're out West? I try to explain all the desert vegetation because hunters usually have never seen it before, and I tell them what it is, how many years it takes to grow, and the like. I try to give them a well-rounded experience instead of having them come out here, shoot an animal, then put them on a plane home. I also try to become friends with these people, because that contributes toward a successful hunt for them, and it also makes it a lot more pleasurable for me. I want them to have an experience, because I know they're going to get a deer.

Carlos Gonzalez Hermosillo: A hunt is successful when the hunter comes and gets what he expects in the way of an experience, the services, the scenario, that atmosphere of adventure. But even when all this is good, I think it comes down to getting the trophy most of the time, or most hunters don't consider it successful. You can give a hunter champagne all day, but if he goes home without his trophy, or at least a legitimate opportunity at one, he's not going to be perfectly happy.

Kirk Kelso: I think if there's good camaraderie, and if there's enjoyment between the hunter and the guide and they've developed a good relationship, and if the opportunities have presented themselves at times during the hunt, then I feel it was a successful hunt, whether or not an animal was taken. The experience needs to be a lot of the enjoyment. If they've had a good time, and they've seen some decent animals, but circumstances caused them not to be able to take one, then I still feel it's a successful hunt.

What is the most common mistake made by guided hunters?

Hal Blood: I think it's coming unprepared, one way or another. They can be unprepared physically, unprepared by not having the right clothing, and so on. Usually their guns are adequate and ready. But I'll tell them what to bring in the way of clothes, and it's like it went in one ear and out the other. Because they didn't listen, it winds up that they're miserable. I don't know why guys do it, but I had one hunter from New Jersey who showed up in cotton duck pants with the nylon front on them, the kind used for upland game hunting. That was after I had clearly told him to bring wools, exactly what footwear to bring, and everything. I tell all my hunters this kind of information, because it's pointless to bring what they use in other places to hunt these big woods. So in essence, the biggest mistake is not following instructions that are designed to prepare them to deal with what they're going to come up against hunting deer in this part of the country.

Jeff Charles: In a nutshell, the most common mistake is not listening to the guide.

Dan Rosman: Probably the most common mistake is not listening to the guide. Once we start guiding up here, I'm busy for a long while, and I see that mistake time after time. The hunters might come up to me after passing up something against the guide's advice, and they want to know what I think. I tell them it sounds like the biggest animal we've seen in a while and I'd have shot it in a heartbeat. So a very common mistake is not listening to the fellow who does this thing for a living.

Chris Pevey: Trying to guide the guide, and having expectations that are too high, are both very common mistakes. I went on a turkey hunt in Alabama this year, and the people there didn't know what I did for a living. The first morning I told them that I didn't have to kill anything, because I was there to have a good time and enjoy the hunt. It was just like a load was lifted off the guide's back. I ended up missing a turkey that morning, too. Hunters need to realize that the guide usually wants them to be successful as much as the hunters want it, and they're most likely giving it all they've got. Unrealistically high expectations of guides really put a lot of pressure on them. It would be great if all hunters would tell their guides at the outset that success would be wonderful, but they're here to have a pleasant time hunting, and learn some things from them, and enjoy the outdoors and the experience together. If a kill comes, it's just icing on the cake.

Charles Ruth: Not paying attention and not following instructions are very common mistakes the hunter makes. A lot of this has to do with mental preparation, which in turn has to do with being comfortable with the firearm. Another common mistake is not being prepared when the big moment arrives and you've got your shot at the animal.

Jay Steen: It's pretty common for guys to get to their hunt destination and not have the proper equipment. I've had people come in without the right clothes, and, amazingly, not even have ammunition with them. Be sure you've got all your stuff, and maybe a little extra. As for mistakes made while on the stand, impatience can defeat them, primarily by leading them to not stay put where they're told to stay. They get up and move around at the wrong time, because they want to see what's around the next bend, and often they miss their opportunity because of it.

David Davis: Not shooting early enough is a common mistake. As I said earlier, it's six seconds of opportunity for a kill out of a six-day hunt. Those seconds could come in the first five minutes of the hunt, or they could come in the last five minutes. The biggest mistake I see guys make comes on the first day when they're just out "looking around" with their guide. They see a giant buck, and they won't shoot! They get greedy, and think that if they can see something that good the first time out, what might they do if they hunt the entire time? Shoot when the opportunity comes, and then the pressure is off them and their guide, and they can go out and really have some fun playing with the deer.

Mike Gardner: Rushing, getting in too big a hurry, is a common mistake that often costs people their chance at a good deer.

Don White: I don't understand this, but some hunters spend all year waiting for a chance to go hunting, and then they want to hunt early in the morning and late in the evening, and go back to camp during the day. Even if you're hunting fourteen or fifteen miles from the house, and you've packed a lunch, they still want to go back to the house regardless of the weather conditions. It's a big mistake, and it boils down to a lazy attitude toward hunting. We want to make them comfortable, of course, but you can be just as comfortable out in the field with a sack lunch as you can be sitting at the table back at the ranch house. I'm kind of a hard-core guy, and I take the areas of the ranch where we're going to be gone all day.

Eric Albus: Not being physically or mentally prepared is a big one. Many come on a physically demanding hunt and they're not prepared by being in shape. Our whitetail hunts aren't so physically demanding, but they still require mental preparation. A lot of guys simply aren't prepared to make the shot when the opportunity presents itself.

Keaton Kelso: Again and again, I say it's a big mistake not to listen to the guide's instructions. When I'm sitting with clients in the stand, there are a few other things I notice. First, they're usually moving way too much. With deer, you're in their bedroom, and you've got to be a statue, or else they're going to catch you. Another thing with my guided hunters is that they pack too much equipment into the field. Some of these guys show up with a 50-pound rucksack filled with all kinds of things they don't need. They also get down out of the stand and go hunting on their own.

There are probably only a handful of people in the country who have killed a B&C deer by sneaking through the woods. But for reasons that escape me, relatively inexperienced hunters seem to think they're going to sneak up on a five- or six-year-old buck and kill him. It's just not going to happen, unless the conditions are exactly right and you're a hunter who really stands out among hunters. I can sit on a stand the week before the client arrives and see thirty to forty deer sometimes. Then I put the client on the stand and he sees nothing. What he's looking for is a total deer standing there, and what you have to search for is an ear flicking or a tail twitching back in the brush. They're just not used to doing that, and too many hunters are simply not capable of seeing something that subtle. It takes patience to be able to do that, and it takes long hours of practice, but the payoff can be incredible.

James Woodley: Scent control, or lack of it, is a big mistake, especially for bow hunters. These hunters have got to get very close to kill a deer, and they need to control scent on their clothing and elsewhere. Another common mistake is not following the recommendations of the guide, say, when he has a stand in mind for them and they've sat there a time or two without seeing anything, so they want to move somewhere else. It comes down to not trusting what your guide says.

Gary Drinkall: Do not hop from stand to stand; this is the number one mistake a hunter can make, and unfortunately the most common. Probably the hardest part

Trust your guide to get you into country where big white-tailed bucks live. (Photo courtesy of Bill Honza)

for the guide is instilling enough confidence in the hunter that the stand is the place to be. Everybody seems to lose hope after a few days of sitting on a stand and not seeing anything big. I understand this problem, and I've been there many times myself, but unfortunately we can't tell the deer where to show up. Hunting whitetails, and guiding for them, is an odds game, and sometimes you come up a winner, and sometimes you lose.

A classic example of lack of patience occurred in our operation just last season. I had scouted an area a great deal and had the stand in position two months before the hunters were to arrive. I even found a monster shed while scouting, and the single antler scored 108. I knew it was a good place, and I'd have a client in there the first day of the season. When my first client arrived, I explained the situation to him, and told him that to get that buck it would take a lot of patience. I put him on the stand, and he hunted there for two days, and saw perhaps fifty deer per day, including quite a few young bucks. He had become bored with the stand, though, and told me he wanted a change of scenery. I told him fine, if that was what he wanted, but I advised him I'd be putting another hunter on that stand if he wasn't going to be on it.

I took him to another stand, where he shortly killed a respectable buck, an old deer that was losing its teeth—a real trophy. Although it was not the monster he wanted, everybody was happy. Meanwhile, the second hunter, whom I put on the stand that the first hunter was on for two days, killed a real monster, the same one whose shed antler I had found! The circumference measurements alone totaled over forty inches, truly the buck of a lifetime, and had the first hunter been patient enough to stay put, it would have been his buck! Underjudging deer is also all too common in our region. These deer have such a big body that most people misjudge the antlers, thinking they're smaller than they really are.

Rene Semple: A really common mistake is not listening to the guides and the advice they give. It's common because a lot of guys who book with us have hunted whitetails their whole lives, like guys from the South. They were weaned on whitetails and they're already good hunters. But when you're in unfamiliar territory, the deer behave differently than they do back home. We know our deer, and even an experienced hunter would be wise to listen to his guide when he's in a new area.

Jim Shockey: One common and serious mistake is not realizing that ultimately they're going to be responsible for their own actions. They pull the trigger because it's their choice. Just because you're on a guided hunt doesn't mean you're on a guaranteed hunt for an X-size animal. Your guide will do his best and tell you what he thinks, but to expect him to be God and look at a deer and say it's exactly this or that score is unfair to the guide. So to me, the most common mistake is to expect the guide to know absolutely, positively at what size animal the hunter's shooting. It may or may not turn out to be what he expected, but then he comes down on the guide if it isn't. Ultimately it was his personal choice. He made the final decision when he pulled the trigger.

Duwane Adams: By far the most common mistake our hunters make is not coming here in good physical condition. One other thing I'd mention is being under-gunned. Let me explain that. Back East, 100 yards is a mile. Well, I've had guys bring .30-30s, .308s, and so on, and have them sighted dead on at 100 yards, because they didn't listen to what I told them. Well, automatically, they've handicapped me! And when I see a deer, they can't kill it, because it's inevitably out of their range, and it's all because they didn't pay attention.

Carlos Gonzalez Hermosillo: Coming to hunt with unrealistic expectations is a common mistake. Too many hunters expect that because they're paying, everything happens automatically without their putting out any effort, any sweat, or any work. It invariably takes some effort to make things happen.

Kirk Kelso: I think the most common mistake clients make is to second-guess the guide or try to control the hunt. They've hired the guide for a reason, and that's to use his expertise and his professionalism, and they need to let him do his job.

What can a guided hunter do that would most improve his chances of taking game (patience, physical fitness, mental preparation, equipment, practice with choice of weapon, and so on)?

Hal Blood: In my hunting, the biggest factor is physical fitness because some days we're going to put in some long treks. Mental preparedness, of course, is a big asset, too.

Jeff Charles: One of the things a person can do is to go out and do some physical preparation, such as walking. Unfortunately, we get a lot of people who come directly from the office to the woods, and they may not have had the time or foresight to get in shape. The other thing I harp on is that it's not good to pick up a rifle once a year and go to the range and shoot, and hope that it's adequate. I recommend that hunters shoot, and shoot often. In this county, you might get only one chance at a deer, and it's pretty disappointing if you can't hit it. The guys who go out the weekend before they come and run four or five shots through the gun, and think they're all right, are just not ready to hunt.

Dan Rosman: Patience is number one, just as it's listed in the question. Physical fitness is important, too, and the hunter really ought to be as ready to hunt as his condition will allow. Mental preparation is big because it can be really cold up here, while you sit all day and see maybe one animal. You need to mentally prepare yourself for that. Equipment ought to fit the hunt, of course. If it's cold where you'll be hunting, you'd better be ready. As for practice, you can't overdo it. Some of the worst hunters in the world have all the high-price rifles and gear, but they don't shoot any until the day before they go on a hunt, and that doesn't usually work. It also helps to have the right rifle. Sometimes we get guys with these really fancy high-dollar guns that are extremely fast and light, but they don't work well on these big deer we have in Michigan.

Chris Pevey: I'm going out to hunt elk in Idaho with my bow soon. I'm getting in shape by walking in the evenings, trying to get as fit as possible. I don't want to be so tired that

Where there are does, bucks are sure to be there, too! (Photo courtesy of Bill Honza)

I can't pull my bow when the time comes. I've got the right equipment, and I practice all the time. I'm also pre-thinking the hunt, asking myself questions like the following: Do I have the right equipment? Can I make the right shot? What situation might develop? When picking a hunt, the hunter needs to become familiar with the kind of terrain where he'll be hunting so that he'll be aware of the situation he's stepping into. Is it swampland, so that he'll need rubber boots and mosquito spray? We like for people to call ahead and ask us what they need to bring along. They also need to know if they'll be hunting deer over an agricultural field or in a dense swamp so that they can have the right rifle caliber. If they do this, they'll be well prepared.

Charles Ruth: In my opinion, mental preparation is the key. That includes being familiar, comfortable, and confident with the weapon. The hunter must also make a real effort to keep alert on the stand at all times. Some people can read a book on the stand and be successful, but for me, I could never get into that!

Jay Steen: Patience is the number one virtue when it comes to improving chances of success. You've got to go deer hunting with an attitude of patience. Don't expect to be on the stand five minutes and fill your tag. Physical fitness doesn't play much of a part in our operation, but it helps to be able to move around a little. Mental preparation involves being ready to sit and wait, and being ready to take the deer when your opportunity comes. You need to know your weapon, and you have to practice enough so that you don't even have to adjust your position to the right eye relief. It ought to be so practiced that when you look through your scope, it's done naturally and automatically.

David Davis: Listen to your guide and shoot when he tells you the opportunity is there. I don't tell my clients when to shoot, but I tell them when not to shoot. I'm not going to let them shoot some three-and-a-half-year-old "pretty boy" that weighs 110 pounds and has a 125-inch set of horns, but looks like he's got 160 up top. If I tell you to shoot, close your eyes to the deer's size and shoot him. I'll suffer the consequences if I'm wrong. So be prepared mentally to shoot when the guide says, "Shoot."

Mike Gardner: In our operation, I see more clients nowadays who are bringing a gun of a caliber that's too heavy. Shot placement is the key. Some people seem to have the attitude that they don't need to make a great shot if they just move up three calibers in size. Shot placement is so important that you need to use a caliber that's in line with what you're hunting. Good binoculars are important, too, the way we hunt here in south Texas, since it's relatively flat so that you can see a long way. We spend about 95 percent of our time looking through binoculars and 5 percent of our time looking through a scope. I'd also recommend a good bipod. When you're out there walking, rattling, stopping, setting up, and looking at incoming bucks, and then you move to another location, a bipod is wonderful. A pair of rattling horns is right up near the top for what we do, too.

Don White: Remaining patient and practicing with the weapon are the top things a hunter can do to improve his

Guides will put the hunter in different situations to get him within range of his buck. (Photo courtesy of Bill Honza)

chances. And don't just go to the range and shoot three times and assume you're ready to hunt. I'm a full-time police officer, and I try to shoot my handguns, as well as my shotguns and rifles, at least once a week. Shooting with any weapon is a learned skill that can be lost if you don't practice. Why spend all that time and money and effort, when it all boils down to just one shot, and you're not ready? Mostly it's confidence in yourself and your weapon, so it's practice, practice, practice.

Eric Albus: Being in good physical shape is a benefit on any hunt, even a relatively easy whitetail hunt. Being mentally prepared is very important, too. Somewhere, sometime, this year, someone is going to be presented with the opportunity of a lifetime, and if he's not prepared to execute the shot, the hunt is going to be a failure. A world-record whitetail comes along only once in a lifetime, and if you blow it, I don't care how good the camp atmosphere and the food and the camaraderie are, you're going to be awfully sick for a long time.

Success has a lot to do with being very comfortable with the weapon you're using. My best rifle hunters and my best archers use one weapon, and they use it extensively. Others come in with a new weapon they have no idea how to use, such as one hunter who came with a new bolt-action rifle he didn't even know how to load. It's a setup for failure. Your weapon is an extension of yourself, and you should be that comfortable with it.

Keaton Kelso: Patience is a big one to improve success rates. A lot of times I've taken hunters into the timber where there's a rub line on trees as big as your thigh and the trunks are completely shredded. The guy will sit on that tree stand one morning and not see anything, so for the afternoon he wants to be moved. I'm enough of a deer hunter to know that I'd live on that tree stand until I saw that buck. Too many people think that if they go on a guided hunt, they're going to see fifteen to twenty bucks every day. In a free-ranging situation, that just doesn't happen. In my area you've had a good day if you see three or four different bucks. People want to bounce around too much just because they didn't see the big guy the first time out. As long as conditions are right with the wind and so on, I'll hunt the same tree stand four or five days straight. If I can do that, eventually the big buck that's using that area will come by there.

James Woodley: My advice to improve your chances is to listen to your guide and then be patient.

Gary Drinkall: Mental preparation is at the top of the list to improve your possibilities. Hunters have to get it into their heads that if they're coming up to British Columbia, it's going to be cold and the hunt is going to require a lot of patience. Lack of mental preparation can lead to a huge, common mistake, namely jumping from stand to stand. I get awfully bored myself looking at the same scenery all the time. But we know, because we've seen it time and time again, that if a guy is hunting in a good place, we're making a huge mistake if we move him prematurely, given a favorable wind and all. We'll go back in a day or two, and there's that buck's track crossing right where we expected him to cross, but he did it while our client was sitting someplace else. Hunters have got to prepare themselves mentally to sit in the cold for a long time, and they must realize that it might not happen this year. If they put their time in, though, eventually everything will go right and they'll get that buck of their dreams.

Rene Semple: Patience and practice are the keys, whether you're using a rifle or a bow. These are tops, in my opinion, for achieving the highest success rates.

Jim Shockey: Hunters should trust their guide to maximize their chance of taking a good buck. When you're on a guided hunt, leave your (usually) inadequate knowledge at home. You can certainly have your own opinions, but generally speaking, in a good area with a good outfitter who has good guides and

Many guides use shooting houses of various types to assure the hunter maximum opportunity to harvest a buck. (Photo courtesy of Bill Honza)

good equipment, you're not going to be qualified to voice a valid opinion on how the hunt is being conducted, what you're doing, nor the choices the guides are making. Don't second-guess him, just trust your guide. You've paid the money and done the research to be in a good area, so just trust him.

Duwane Adams: Every one of them is included in the question, and each one of those things needs to be underlined. Practice is underemphasized. What I tell hunters to do is take a paper plate and put it at 360 yards, shoot and see where you hit, and then move and do it from a different place. You've got to get very efficient with that weapon to maximize your chances of success. If you aren't, you can do everything else right and miss when you get the opportunity.

Carlos Gonzalez Hermosillo: I think it's important for hunters to learn as much as they can about the species they're hunting and to know what a trophy looks like. They shouldn't expect the guide to do all the judging of trophy quality; they should have some idea of their own. I do this with any animal I'm hunting. I get out the record books and read all about any animal I'm going to hunt. I don't necessarily use it to get my name in the book as much as I enjoy reading the really good information that's there about all kinds of animals. A hunter can improve his experience and his chances of success by doing this.

Kirk Kelso: I think absolutely the most important thing, especially in hunting Coues deer, is to be proficient with the rifle, to be a real rifleman. The client doesn't have to be the best hunter in the world, because that's why he's hired the guide. He wants the guide to be the hunter, to be able to find the animal, and to get him in a situation to kill it. If he's enough of a rifleman when his chance comes, that's probably the most important thing.

Besides the weapon, what is the most important single piece of equipment every hunter should carry?

Hal Blood: Up here, the single most important piece of equipment is a compass. Usually my hunters are with me, but we could split up, or something could happen to me, and without a compass it's impossible to navigate here. When we leave camp, I tell the other guides where we're going and where we're heading, but a compass is a pretty important piece of equipment in the big woods. Most people are used to hunting in a forty- to one-hundred-acre wood lot, and up here we don't relate to that, because we'll walk through a hundred acres in less than ten minutes sometimes. I have them bring a belt pack, and in it they're to have their compass, their lunch, a knife, some matches, and the like.

Jeff Charles: The most important single piece of equipment up here in Maine is undoubtedly a compass. I try to get all my hunters to put together a little pack to carry, and it always includes a compass. Another thing is plenty of water, because I'm really big on staying hydrated. People say they're not hot and they're not thirsty, so they don't drink enough and they really dry out. I've seen a lot of guys who have gotten in trouble because of this. We also take with us a small first aid kit, matches, and a survival blanket, just in case you have to spend a night in the woods. You don't want to overweight yourself with a lot of stuff, but those few things can make the difference between being comfortable or not.

Dan Rosman: Matches are perhaps the most important thing to have with you in cold country. You also ought to have some snacks, such as candy, with you. I've been in situations where I've gone a while without anything to eat. If a hunter has any type of medication that he's got to have, I don't care if he's just going out back for a little while, he's got to have it with him. We had a situation where a fellow was allergic to bees and he didn't have his medicine with him to counter a sting, and that one didn't turn out the best way. That kind of stuff you've got to have. I'd recommend matches, candy, a flashlight, and other things that will help you survive for a while if necessary.

Chris Pevey: Footwear is a huge item, as far as I'm concerned. If you can't walk because of blisters, or if you need rubber boots and you've got walking boots, or whatever, you're in trouble. Find out ahead of time so you can bring the right footwear. If you're sitting in a stand, will you have enough clothes to stay warm? Find out the answers to these questions so you'll be comfortable, because the longer you can stay on stand the better your chances of success.

Charles Ruth: Again, understand that I dealt exclusively with stand hunting when I was actively guiding. Within reason, you should have with you anything that is going to increase your comfort and allow you to concentrate and stay on the stand as long as it's going to take. I don't know if I can come up with an individual piece of equipment that's suitable for everybody, because it could be as simple as a truly comfortable seat cushion for some people. For others it could be something to snack on, something to drink, or whatever.

Jay Steen: The right clothing for the hunting situation is pretty important. If you're cold, you're going to be moving around, and if you're too hot, you'll be uncomfortable and probably moving around, too. Next, good binoculars would be something that you'd definitely need, especially hunting stands like we do. We have some people that we hunt out of their own climbing stands, and you sure need to know how to operate your stand if you do that.

David Davis: Good binoculars is the answer to both questions.

Mike Gardner: I think having too much equipment is a hindrance. I have some clients who bring so much equipment that they spend all their time keeping up with their gear. I go back to good binoculars and a good bipod. I like those spotting scopes that are mounted on a rifle stock, too, with a sling on it that you can throw over your back. When you stop, you can pull that spotting scope off your back and look through it like looking through a riflescope. We all have spotting scopes mounted on rifle stocks, and we all really like the way it works in the field. Cabela's sells these now, and it's really nice. For us, it makes it much easier to do a quick field judging of a buck. We use ours a lot when we're out riding, and we can just throw it up and take a quick look.

The work begins after the shot, and the hunter should pitch in to get the job done expeditiously. (Photo courtesy of Bill Honza)

Don White: I'm a gadget guy, and I've bought it all. When it comes down to it, though, and I'm getting serious about hunting, I take only my rifle and binoculars. That's it. Everything else stays in the truck. You can't compensate for poor woodsmanship with technology. The fewer gadgets you have to worry about, the better off you'll be. Spend your money on your rifle and your optics.

Eric Albus: For the archery hunter, a rangefinder is the most important piece of equipment. Don't leave home without one, because rangefinders have been the biggest advance in the archery world since the invention of the compound bow. For the trophy rifle hunter, it's optics, both in the riflescope and binoculars. You can get by with a cheaper rifle, because most off-the-shelf rifles shoot better in the field than the shooter can, even if they're the cheapest rifles made and they're right out of the box. But don't skimp on your scope or your binoculars. They can make the difference between a trophy whitetail and a disappointing mistake, and the difference between going home happy and going home disgusted.

Keaton Kelso: The most critical piece of equipment depends on whether you're using a bow or a rifle. A shooting stick is something we recommend for rifle hunters. Scent-lock clothes are highly recommended, especially for muzzleloader and archery hunters, but they're also important for rifle hunters. One of the most essential pieces of equipment is a pair of binoculars. Too many people will go out and buy a $1,000 rifle and a $500 scope, and then they go to Wal-Mart and buy $50 binoculars. Optics is what makes this business successful for a lot of guys. Those who spend the money on good optics can see animals others can't see. It is so essential to spend the money on optics, so you can see well into the brush.

James Woodley: A rangefinder is really big for bowhunting. That's especially true when you're going on a guided hunt. You could even wind up hunting ten different stands on a five-day hunt, so it's nothing like hunting your own stand where you know how far away every tree is.

Gary Drinkall: I think everybody should carry good optics. Some guys come on a hugely expensive hunt and bring $35 binoculars! It doesn't have to be top of the line, but a hunter should bring a decent set of glasses, because there are bad mistakes made by looking at a deer through terrible binoculars. Another thing I like is for a guy to take a thermos of some kind for a hot drink—coffee, tea, or whatever—so that he can take a little drink from time to time and warm up and relax. First aid and emergencies aren't really a factor because it's all stand hunting and we're in close contact, so it comes down to being able to see well and stay comfortable and warm all day.

Rene Semple: We make sure our hunters have the right stuff, and we're in radio contact with them all the time. We really baby-sit our hunters so that they don't lack for anything, even if they didn't bring it. All of our stands are box blinds, either on the ground or elevated, and all have heaters. We check on them all the time, and if anything's not right they can call us. We want to make sure they're not cold, because if you get cold you'll miss things. We want them nice and comfortable so that they'll put in the time and stay sharp while they're doing it.

Jim Shockey: I don't think there's any question that the most essential item is good binoculars. Beyond the binoculars, a hunter needs good hiking boots that aren't going to leave you in any way dysfunctional on the hunt. From there you go on down the equipment list.

Duwane Adams: Most people would say binoculars, but let me tell you, it's boots. Most people buy a brand-new pair of boots, and sometimes they try them on the day they get here, sometimes a week before they get here. They're crippled right off the bat. It's a horrible situation when that happens. I carry an assortment of foot remedies in my backpack, everything from moleskin to NewSkin. I've got all kinds of stuff because if the hunter's crippled, he can't hunt! Boots are therefore *the* number one piece of equipment for Coues deer hunting. Most people who hunt here come from back East, and they're used to walking a hundred yards and climbing into their tree stand. Out here they're going up and down hills, slipping and sliding, and jamming their toes. I've had guys who were black and blue and had their toenails fall off.

Carlos Gonzalez Hermosillo: Good binoculars, without question, on both counts. I also count a good Swiss Army knife as among the important things to carry on any hunt.

Kirk Kelso: In the Coues deer game, you need to have good, high-quality optics. You need to have a tripod to set the optics on because you're going to be glassing over extended distances for long periods of time. I think binoculars and a good spotting scope are the most important things besides the rifle, because you're going to spend 90 percent of your time behind the optics.

Are there any common items of equipment that you feel are unnecessary, redundant, or just plain worthless for hunting whitetails?

Hal Blood: Yeah, a lot of them! The number one thing would be a Global Positioning System (GPS). To me it's just something extra to carry, and most of the time the hunters are just fooling around with it. They mark where the truck is, and they depend on the device too much. A compass is much simpler, and you don't have to give it any attention until you need it. Another thing that people often have is a sling on their rifle, and if they do have one, I make them take it off. If you've got your rifle on a sling, you're not ready to shoot. Slings are always getting caught on brush and then snapping it back. I don't mind if hunters take their slings off and put them in their packs because a sling can come in pretty handy when you're dragging a deer.

Jeff Charles: There's so much stuff on the market, and I have hunters who come with everything imaginable. If they believe it helps them, good! I've got a man who hunts with us who just spent $150 for a box to take the scent out of his clothes. For no money, I can hang mine outside and do the same thing, but it made him happy, so I didn't knock what he'd bought. Scents are good, but if you work with the wind in your favor, you don't need them. Some things aren't worthless, some are better than others, and some just don't fit our hunting situation.

Dan Rosman: The only thing I can think of is some of the scents that people bring. If the scent isn't native to the area, you might as well just throw it away. I've let clients put it out, and I told them, "OK, we'll try it." There might not be a scent anything like it native to the area, and the deer will turn tail and run when he smells it.

Chris Pevey: I read that question and I just cracked up! You don't have enough pages for me to answer this one! I've

These Kansas hunters had a great day of hunting with their guides. (Photo courtesy of Keaton Kelso)

had people show up with backpacks full of stuff, and they need to have the right stuff, but you need to sift it down to the essentials. I've had people break out headphones and listen to college football while we're on the stand. Well, that's not me! Most of my guides carry some extra gear in case the hunter forgets something. Take enough to be comfortable, but don't overdo it.

Charles Ruth: Here in South Carolina, the most unnecessary item would be a spotting scope. Most hunters are going to have binoculars, but there's absolutely no need for a spotting scope here. In our situation, I really don't see a whole lot of use even for binoculars. The hunter sees a deer, he throws his binoculars up, and guess what? He should have been looking through the riflescope because in our dense habitat, by the time he switches to the rifle, the deer is gone and he's missed his chance. But unless he's lugging a huge backpack full of stuff, anything the hunter wants to take is pretty much OK with me.

Jay Steen: Here we don't have a lot of 500-yard shots, so you can probably leave your rangefinders at home. The little powder-puff things that show you the way the wind is coming from aren't much help when you're sitting on a stand. Cover scents can be left at home. If a deer smells human scent, it doesn't matter what it's mixed with, he's out of there.

David Davis: I believe certain items are unnecessary. For instance, I'm not big on cover scents. You can't hide your smell from a whitetail with cover scents. On the other hand, I will admit I'm a gadget guy. I've got all the gadgets, and I like all of them, so I don't consider any of them worthless.

Mike Gardner: Nothing comes to mind.

Don White: On our ranch you can leave the scents out, and you can usually leave the grunt calls at home. You're not going to pull a buck off a hot doe's scent, and you know how bucks walk when they're on a mission. If you're rattling, you might grunt once in a while. Honestly, scent is not as important on our ranch as it might be on other ranches. A whitetail uses its nose as its number one danger detector, but on our ranch about 50 percent of the deer come in from downwind, and that's the truth. When guys leave the ranch, they leave their scents behind, and I've got a whole closet full of various ones. I've also got a lot of special hunting junk they left here because they realized they didn't need it. It's unusual, but on our ranch whitetails don't seem to associate man's scent with danger because there's so little pressure on them. In most places scent control is absolutely key to success, but this is not the case on our ranch.

Eric Albus: I'm not much of a fan of gimmick items and gadgets. Most items of this nature that people bring on a hunt are fairly worthless.

Keaton Kelso: There's every gadget out there, and some guys will show up with a 50-pound rucksack filled with all of them. My personal feeling is that you're there to hunt. Take your rifle and shells, shooting sticks, optics, maybe a rangefinder, and that's really all you need to pack. I've actually sat all day with clients after they've carried that thing along over really rough terrain. It's exhausting for them. That first evening after we get back to camp, we'll set that bag down on the table and go through it with them. I'll tell them they don't need this, they don't need that, and so on, and when it comes right down to it they don't even need the bag! If you can carry it in a little fanny pack on your side, that's all you need.

I had a guy last year bring a scent-lock system that was like a pair of waders, and it took twenty to thirty minutes to put them on and take them off, and he was sweating by the time he got to the stand, and probably put out more scent than he would have without that outfit. It's probably different in elk country, but out here survival isn't usually an issue, and the more stuff you take in with you, the more you stink.

James Woodley: I really don't have anything in mind, but some of the gimmick calls and scents don't seem to be worth much. I'm not saying they never work, but they don't seem to be consistent enough in producing the desired effect to be worth the price.

Gary Drinkall: Some scents work and some scents don't, but I'm not a scent fan. I had a guy up last year who worked two different stands where hunters were seeing five or six bucks a night. He went out and helped the guide re-bait the area, and while he was doing that he sprinkled some of his bottled scent around all over the place. It shut those stands down for three days, and we didn't see a deer during that time, not even a doe. We figure it was the scent he put out. People can be overzealous with scents. I really don't mind a cover scent to mask the human smell while you're going into the stand, but people tend to overspray that stuff and generally overuse it. Calls aren't worthless, but you've got to know how to use them or you're better off leaving them at home.

Rene Semple: I've seen a lot of gadgets come through, but I honestly can't say that any one stands out as totally worthless.

Jim Shockey: Well, my apologies to the manufacturers, but about 99 percent of the junk out there that is sold to hunters is close to worthless.

Duwane Adams: Most hunters come overdressed because it's cold where they come from—New Jersey or Minnesota or Wisconsin—and they come with wool or some other heavy fabric that's appropriate for brutal weather; you don't need that when hunting Coues deer in Arizona. I've told them on the phone that they shouldn't overdress, because it can be freezing in the morning and in the 70s in two hours. Soon they've got their backpacks full of clothes, and clothes tied around their waists, and they're still burning up. They only do this for the first day or two, and then they learn. It's common sense to dress in layers of lighter fabrics, but some people have got to see it done before they understand it.

Carlos Gonzalez Hermosillo: Sometimes people bring very strange equipment. I've had people bring a minus-75-degree parka on a mountain hunt in the desert for Coues whitetails. We do need a jacket, but not anything that heavy. Good mountain boots for walking on a hill sideways are a real necessity, too, but you've got to get a good fit and have them broken in or you'll end your hunt with sore feet.

Kirk Kelso: If there is any piece of equipment that the hunter is not familiar with enough so that he can put it to use to aid him in hunting, then it's an item he ought to leave in camp. For instance, last season we had quite a few clients show up with the new shooting sticks with three legs. Two-legged shooting sticks work very well if you use them correctly, but if a guy isn't used to it, getting the two legs down and setting up the device is tough enough in the field. Trying to get three legs down, and then get them set up and leveled so that we were on the animal, was an absolute mess every time we had those in the field. The point is that if you're not accustomed to using something, don't bring it. Whatever hunters bring, they should use like the safety on their rifles; that is, they should be so accustomed to using their equipment that they do it without even having to think about it. If a guy knows how to use his gear well, so that it's second nature to him, there's very little I'd call worthless.

Chapter 6
HUNTING BIG-WOODS BUCKS

Describe your home guiding area for whitetails. What are some distinctions that set it apart?

Hal Blood: I call the type of whitetail hunting we do here in northern Maine mountainous, big-woods hunting. There are large tracts of nonagricultural land here, with mountains everywhere, big draws, and steep hillsides. What sets it apart is that there are lower deer densities but also lower hunter densities, and the body size of the deer is among the largest on the continent. Additionally, we have some of the harshest winters here, even for Maine. We get the earliest snow, and spring comes the latest of anywhere in Maine.

Jeff Charles: The big-woods area of Maine has a lot of cutover land because the paper companies are really cutting hard up here right now. There are a lot of major blowdowns and some tough walking. The deer in Maine have come back well, and with this terrain they have the advantage now. A lot of people think it's going to be open country, but a lot of times when you do shoot a deer, you can't even see the whole animal. The elevation ranges from 1,000 feet to 2,500 feet, and that's a pretty significant elevation change, even though the altitude isn't very high. We can start out on bare ground and wind up hunting in the snow. The distinctive features are that it's big country, it isn't hunted very heavily, there's virtually no farmland, and it has the biggest deer in Maine. If you want to shoot just any deer, go to southern Maine. If you want to shoot a big deer, this is the place to do it, because the deer have to be big and strong to survive the hard winters here.

Dan Rosman: In Michigan, we've got a lot of big oaks, hardwoods, and so on, and a lot of big cedar swamps. In among all this we have a lot of agricultural fields mixed in. It's rolling

Northern deer inhabit cold, snowy country during the hunting season. (Photo courtesy of Bill Honza)

This great Michigan buck was taken after a hard hunt by this satisfied hunter. (Photo courtesy of Bill Honza)

hills with no really high terrain. My main guiding area is about 4,000 acres. The distinctive feature of my area is its cedar swamps, where there are a lot of dark little holes where the deer like to hide. Any time there's any pressure at all, that's where the deer head.

Why should a hunter hire a guide, as opposed to being self-guided?

Hal Blood: If they've never hunted in this type of area, they're really going to be totally clueless. They're going to be overwhelmed right from the start. They'll get out of their vehicles and not even know where to start. They should at least hire a guide for a year or two just to learn how to hunt here, and then they might be able to go on their own. Every year we have people drop in who have rented lodging locally, and then they show up here looking for a guide when they realize they don't know what the heck they're doing.

Jeff Charles: I think the main thing is that the hunter is getting immediate knowledge. If a person wants to go on a self-guided hunt, and he has the time, that's fine. But if you've only got five or six days, that guide should be doing the work for you in finding where to hunt. That's going to multiply your chance of success many times over.

Dan Rosman: I think the biggest reason is that most guys just don't have enough time to do enough scouting. The guides are there year-round, and they eat, sleep, and dream deer hunting. They just know where the animals are likely to be. A lot of our clients simply don't have the time to do that. The guide is your scout, and he'll take you straight to the place where you need to start hunting.

A hunter approaches a downed giant after hunting hard in the big woods. (Photo courtesy of Bill Honza)

Steve Comus and guide Dan Rosman admire a hard-won prize from the big woods. (Photo courtesy of Bill Honza)

What is your success rate on trophy animals?

Hal Blood: I don't know. Successful hunts run close to 100 percent, but not all of the successes involve kills. We keep perpetuating the erroneous notion that success is killing something. I don't keep track of the percentage numbers, which can involve not just kills, but also opportunities, misses, etc.

Jeff Charles: We never guarantee a hunter a deer, of course, because what we're selling is a total experience. What I tell potential clients is that if they give me five years, I'll get them a 200-pound buck. To a great degree, though, it depends on the person. I've had people come up here who will probably never shoot a deer in their lives, at least not in our area. I've got other guys who will shoot a big deer every year or every other year. So much depends on experience level, even for a guided hunter. I'm not avoiding the question, but defining the success rate is really tough in this part of the country.

Dan Rosman: I'd like to say around 80 percent on opportunity, with about a 50 percent kill rate.

Describe your usual hunting method and any common variations.

Hal Blood: 90 percent of what we do is either tracking or still-hunting. If there's snow, we're tracking, and if there's no snow, we're still-hunting, easing along slowly, stopping a lot and looking for deer. When we get on a hot buck track, we stay on it until we catch up to him.

Jeff Charles: First, I size up a new guy and see what he's capable of doing. I have to decide if he's a stand hunter, a still hunter, or whatever. Then I have to adapt to the client's ability level. I try to accommodate the client. If the client says he wants to go into a warm place for lunch, that's what we do. It's his trip, and he's the one who's paying for it. If he wants to be out there from daylight until dark, going all day long, we'll

Guide Hal Blood's big-woods buck taken in typical northern conditions. (Photo courtesy of Hal Blood)

do that, too. Generally, I like to put inexperienced hunters on a stand, get them way back where they're going to see a deer if they hang tough. So again, the hunting method varies with the individual.

If a guy wants to get up into the snow and really go after one of those big boys, we start out early on a fresh track, and we go until we catch up. The deer is going to go into the wind, so you naturally work the wind. If you can get on the deer early enough and push him a couple of times, you can determine his pattern. If you determine what he's going to do when you push him, and you know the terrain, generally you can get a look at him.

Dan Rosman: I normally get out into the woods an hour before daylight and sit either in a blind or whatever, and then I still-hunt all day. I move along with a client really slowly, and we go right into the thick stuff. We take two or three steps and stop and glass and wait. The biggest deer we ever kill, we do it this way. I'm fortunate to hunt with a lot of hunters who have come back year after year, and they know how I do it. We get in there and just barely move, easing along looking for any sign of a deer.

Do you use any special techniques, such as rattling, grunting, or a doe-in-heat lure?

Hal Blood: We use them a little bit. I rattle some the first week of the season if it's a calm morning and the woods are noisy. I carry a rattling bag that first week. I carry a grunt call, but the only time I use it is if I know there's a deer around, if I jump one, or if I hear one snort. I don't walk around grunting, though.

Jeff Charles: I try to have all my hunters carry a grunt call. It won't bring the deer in, but it's a great way to stop a deer. I've had many hunters on a stand toot on that grunt call when they see a deer. The deer stops, simply because it's curious, and often the hunter can then get in a good shot. I've done some rattling, usually early in the season. We don't have a high ratio of bucks to does in this area, so it doesn't work as well as where there are more bucks.

A camp scene in Maine's big woods. (Photo courtesy of Hal Blood)

Dan Rosman: We rattle quite a bit when the time is right, and it's effective. I love grunting, too. There are lots of times when I'll just grunt without rattling at all. It seems like up here you get about a one-week period when rattling works, but with grunting you can really have some good success over a longer period of time. I've been out with some great people, like Bill Jordan, and a few years ago we grunted in a buck with just a grunt tube, and it was something to see. I haven't had much luck using doe-in-heat lure, even though a lot of guys swear by it.

How do you hunt differently with a client/hunter, as opposed to when hunting alone?

Hal Blood: When I have my clients I do pretty much the same as when I'm on my own. I just have to keep in mind that my limiting factor in mobility is the client, because some get around better than others. Other than that, my techniques are not a heck of a lot different.

Jeff Charles: I can't sit on a stand unless I'm bowhunting. I like to go after the deer and stay on my feet all day long. If I know there's a big buck in the area, I move very slowly, and I might not go more than a mile or a mile and a half in a whole day. When I find a place where there's a big buck, I like to sneak in and sneak out. I don't like to stay in there and get my scent all over the place and push him several times, like I might do with a client.

Dan Rosman: It's about the same. The only thing is that when I'm by myself I move even slower. I don't mind sitting for an awfully long time or just barely moving. If I know something is around there, my thinking is just to be patient and slow.

What time of the season offers the best hunting in your area [and the highest possibility of success on trophy animals]?

Hal Blood: Any time we have snow is excellent. Which week doesn't matter nearly as much as conditions that week, and snow

Maine's big woods seldom yield a 300-pound buck without tremendous effort and commitment. (Photo courtesy of Jeff Charles)

is ideal for tracking. The rut does influence finding tracks, because they're moving around more and you can always find a track if there's snow. The season is basically November, and the rut is the last half of the month. But presence or absence of snow is the most important factor by far.

Jeff Charles: We've only got four weeks of hunting, basically all of November, and the last week nobody will come because it's Thanksgiving. The first week can be really good, because nobody has pushed the deer yet, and they're not quite as wary, so a lot of times that first week can be the best. The rut begins toward the end of the first week and goes into the second week. The last week we usually have more snow. Some years, during the last week, the rut is winding down, and we sometimes see two or three bucks together. To me, all four weeks of our Maine season are equally good.

Dan Rosman: It's during the rut, which occurs up here in October. That's when their defenses are down, and that's about the only time. The bucks are thinking about the opposite sex, and that's what gets them.

How much does weather influence hunting success in your area?

Hal Blood: Snow is what really helps us out the most, and we'll kill more deer when we have snow than when we don't. Colder weather really helps out a lot, too. Even rain to keep it quiet and a little cooler is a big help.

Jeff Charles: Weather is big. I can't tell you exactly what the figures are, but when we have a snowstorm in Maine, the kill figures definitely go up. Inexperienced hunters can't see a track on bare ground, and I've had hunters claim after a few days of hunting that there are no deer here. We then get a few inches of snow, and they want to know where all the deer came from, because the tracks are everywhere and they're easy to see. When you get snow, even the inexperienced hunter can follow tracks. Rain is good, too, and I love to hunt in the rain, so long as it's not a driving rain. We also have several days each season when it's dangerous to be in the woods because it's blowing and snowing and you've got trees coming down. If you're afraid to be in the woods, so are the deer, and they really hunker down somewhere.

Dan Rosman: If we get a lot of snow late in the season, it brings them more to the edges of the fields, and they'll ball up into groups a little more when it's really cranking down. But the only thing that really negatively affects the hunting is high wind and heavy rain. When you get rain or wind, it's tough, tough hunting.

How much does weather/ time of season influence where and how you hunt in your area?

Hal Blood: It doesn't really affect it at all. I always hunt where I know there's a big buck, and everything else is secondary.

Jeff Charles: Generally, in nasty, blowing weather, you have to hunt the thick places because that's where the deer are lying. In that kind of weather, some people don't want to hunt because they think the deer are in such thick stuff that you'll never be able to see them. But they bed down right out in the open so that they can see, usually on a knoll with the wind in their faces so that they can slip out a back door. If you can get in on them, you can see them.

Dan Rosman: If it's early in the season and it's hot, I get right down in those cedar swamps, where they tend to ball up by the water. It's cool there. Late in the season I work the field edges, especially if there's lots of snow. They tend to like the field edges, and they get on that edge, and they're a little bit easier to pattern, it seems.

Chapter 7

HUNTING OLD SOUTH BUCKS

Describe your home guiding area for whitetails. What are some distinctions that set it apart?

Chris Pevey: We're broken down into three basic types of areas. We have creek swamps, with some sixteen miles bordering Briar Creek, a tributary of the Savannah River, and we have about seventeen miles of frontage on the river itself. Along these are big hardwood swamp areas. We also have stands on agricultural fields. The third type of terrain is upland food plots and pinewoods. Most of our guided hunts are on food plots, because there we have ample time to judge the deer and make a good, solid shot. It's a place where you usually don't have to make a split-second decision about a buck. The area is distinctive because of its sheer size, which on Millhaven is 24,000 contiguous acres, one of the biggest such parcels east of the Mississippi River. That gives us a lot of huntable acres.

In addition, we've been on QDM (Quality Deer Management) for over twenty years, and the age class of our bucks is higher than in most places. We kill a lot of 4½-year-olds, 5½-year-olds, and even older bucks. When you come onto Millhaven, you don't see a lot of deer, but you see a good percentage of *quality* deer. Our doe numbers are way down because we kill about four hundred does per year and about forty bucks per year. We've got about a 1:2 buck-to-doe ratio. During the rut, these deer act like deer ought to act, and the grunt call works, and rattling horns work. When you come here, you get to see a lot of bucks of different age classes, so you can learn how to judge them. You see a lot of 120 to 130 B&C class deer here, like nowhere else in Georgia.

Guide Charles Ruth with an excellent South Carolina buck. (Photo courtesy of Charles Ruth)

Charles Ruth: We're in the lower Coastal Plain of South Carolina, where there are a lot of commercial pine plantations. They're laced with hardwood drains, and at Cedar Knoll there's a major river flood plain, too. There is a good mix of wildlife openings, food plots, and firing lanes, and all of it is in the midst of exceptional deer habitat with a lot of natural forage. The habitat is distinguished by the density of its vegetation, its briars and the like. There is relatively low visibility unless you're on a wildlife opening or a prepared firing lane. People have a hard time visualizing how dense our Southeastern clear-cuts can become when they're covered in five- to-seven-year-old pine plantations.

Jay Steen: We're right on the edge of what's called the Black Belt area of Alabama, a place famous for its big Southeastern deer. Our place is all river-bottom land, situated on the Tombigbee River. It's flat, but it's really a very diverse habitat, with everything from cutover areas to planted pines of different ages to hardwood bottoms where the trees are up to a hundred years old. It's unique for the Southeast because of the size of the block of land we have, 10,000 acres. We have an ongoing timber operation all year long, except during deer season, and that's what creates so much diversity. Each one of our hunters has several options every day as to what kind of area he wants to hunt.

Why should a hunter hire a guide, as opposed to being self-guided?

Chris Pevey: A guide knows the land, the terrain, what the deer are doing at that time, whether it's the rut, how the phase of the moon affects the deer, and where the travel areas and feeding areas are located. He's in tune with what's going on with the deer when the hunter arrives. A guy who just walks onto a place is handicapped from the start. A guide is exactly that, he's a guide. He's there to show you where and how to hunt. I'm going elk hunting this fall, and I can tell you that the first thing I did was find the best guide I could locate for the money. Having a good guide simply increases your percentage of success, hands down.

Charles Ruth: I wouldn't even recommend that a local person hire a guide. We've dealt with relatively few instate hunters at Cedar Knoll. As for out-of-state hunters, they've already made the decision that they're going to go elsewhere, that they want to see some different country, and it's a place unfamiliar to them. Even being a guide, if I go somewhere else to hunt, I want a guide. It's going to cost you a pretty good chunk to go on a trip, so in my opinion you ought to go all the way and bear the extra expense of a good guide who knows the place and has on-the-ground experience there.

Who knows what superb bucks are still out there? (Photo courtesy of Bill Honza)

Jay Steen: In the Southeast, a guide contributes to the quality of the hunt, as well as to safety. You can come to Alabama and hunt on a public management area, and there are plenty of them, but you don't know where to go, and you don't know who else is in the woods with you. A guide isn't required here, but it's the best option for both success and safety.

What is your success rate on trophy animals?

Chris Pevey: Our success rate is near 100 percent. We take 40 guys out each year and we take 40 bucks.

Charles Ruth: It's hard to say what our success rate is. We were very high on harvest at Cedar Knoll, because I dealt with almost three thousand harvested animals during the years I was guiding, and thousands and thousands of man-days of hunting. Here's what I would tell you: Most people would consider a 100-point buck in South Carolina a very nice buck. I would say we probably took in the neighborhood of two hundred twenty-five to two hundred fifty bucks like that. I've hunted in five states for whitetails, and I can tell you that these coastal bucks in South Carolina are some of the toughest to take. Some of that has to do with the length of our season, which is 140 days. These are pressured animals, and when they turn two and a half years old you can't get away with anything with them.

Jay Steen: We run between 30 and 40 percent on kills, and 50 to 60 percent or more on opportunities.

Describe your usual hunting method and any common variations.

Chris Pevey: That depends on several variables. Say a guy is here on a full moon, for example. We might not go out really early that morning unless I've got a good sitter. If he's a little antsy, we might go out at 10:00 A.M. and sit until 2:00 P.M. If the acorns have all been eaten, we'll work the food plots. We're going to work the deer wherever they're most likely to be. It also depends on who you're guiding. If you've got a guy who can't use a climber, you're going to have to figure out something that will work for him. Maybe you get into a good travel area so that you can put up a tripod on a road. Feeding areas are great when the acorns are dropping, so you can set up a climber or a ground blind. Your whole setup is based on following deer movement, plus the hunter's capabilities.

Charles Ruth: Typically, in the morning we'd put the hunter into the maximum amount of cover on a stand that takes advantage of a cut shooting lane. Mornings are a woods situation, usually. During the rut the animals crisscross these places repeatedly chasing does, and they also move through feeding on natural vegetation, and these locations are productive. In the afternoons we lean more toward a typical planted food plot, generally linear in configuration, and we catch the deer feeding. The morning hunt relies more on a random-movement situation, while the evening hunt relies on feeding. As a general thing, figuring out a deer's nose and what it's eating will get you where you need to be most of the time.

Jay Steen: We normally hunt the mornings out of fixed stands in hardwood bottoms, tripods overlooking cutover areas, or "hub and spoke" areas where we've cut shooting lanes in thick, middle-aged pine stands. We will hunt people out of their own climbing stands if they want. We try to hunt them in places away from the fixed stands. In the afternoon we hunt on or around food plots. We mix it up according to deer movements, and we'll move back into the acorn bottoms in the evening if that's where the deer are.

Do you use any special techniques such as rattling, grunting, or a doe-in-heat lure?

Chris Pevey: I'm not a big fan of scents, but I'm definitely a grunter and a rattler, especially during the rut. Rattling works best during the rut, but I use a grunt call every time we go out, three times about every fifteen minutes. I'm just trying to catch a buck out there that I can't see and bring him in.

A superb Alabama buck taken at Westervelt Lodge. (Photo courtesy of Jay Steen)

The only lure I'm a big fan about is a household item, and that's vanilla extract. If you want to kill a doe, put some of that on a cotton ball and set it up, and they'll come in like raccoons. They like that sweet smell. Persimmon scent works the same way. As for buck lure, I've noticed that the smaller bucks will come in to that, but the older bucks are a little bit smarter. I'm not saying it won't work; it's just that it doesn't seem to work well for me. But grunting and rattling are definitely effective, and they also add excitement to the hunt.

Charles Ruth: The hunter is welcome to try these things if they want. My job as a guide is to have recent knowledge of deer in the area and get the hunters in the right spot as far as the wind is concerned. Beyond that, if the hunter wants to put out some lure or try some rattling or grunting, that's

A Georgia buck taken with a well-traveled Remington .30-06. (Photo courtesy of Chris Pevey)

Guide Chris Pevey with an outstanding Millhaven Plantation buck. (Photo courtesy of Chris Pevey)

fine with me. Personally, I don't use many of these techniques, because if the deer can smell the doe-in-heat lure, they've long ago smelled you, too. To me it's better to get the wind right, get in the right place, and then be a fly on the wall.

Jay Steen: We've had success rattling right at the beginning of the rut. A lot of people talk about having success grunting, stopping deer and actually getting them to come back. Sometimes the doe-in-heat lure works; we've had people drag it behind them on the way to the stand, and then a buck walks right up to them. As for cover scents, we don't do a lot of that.

How do you hunt differently with a client/hunter, as opposed to when hunting alone?

Chris Pevey: I don't change any of the main points. I give it 110 percent, whether I've got a hunter with me or not. Your setup might be a little different, but it's because with two people in the stand you've got to make twice as sure the wind is right. You're not going to get away with anything when you've got

Wes Vining took this Georgia buck at Cypress Creek, the author's place in Georgia.

another guy in the stand with you hunting whitetails. I'm a scent-control freak, and I'll pick a stand where the wind is coming right into my face. Another thing I do differently is to teach my hunters some things and make it an instructional experience so that they get more bang for their buck. If the guy thinks he knows more than me, we'll meet in the middle somewhere.

Charles Ruth: Since I am an archer and I primarily guide rifle hunters, I naturally do some things differently for myself out of necessity. I have to get the deer much closer for myself than I do for a client with a rifle.

Jay Steen: I rarely ever get to hunt for myself anymore. Most of my hunting is hunting places for other people to hunt. I'm not an active hunter anymore, but I was before I got into this business.

Guide Chris Pevey with a terrific bow-killed Georgia buck.

What time of the season offers the best hunting in your area (and the highest possibility of success on trophy animals)?

Chris Pevey: Here we have three distinct rut peaks, and they're all great. The first week of deer season in late October is really good, with a very high success rate, and they're in full-blown rut then. There's another peak around Thanksgiving that is also excellent.

Charles Ruth: For any place you hunt, practically, there's going to be the "opening day" phenomenon, but understand our opening day is in August, in late summer. The deer are naïve for the first week, and then it gets really tough for a while. From the last week in September through the middle of October, you get a lot of pre-rut activity leading up to the breeding season, and it can be really good hunting. Then from October 15 to November 15 the rut is on, and that's usually a good time. Everybody wants to hunt the rut, but the time leading up to the rut is also an excellent time, because the bucks are ready and the does aren't, and the bucks move around an awful lot then trying to find a receptive female.

Jay Steen: The rut is best. We start seeing rut activity in mid-December, and it continues through mid-January. Early in the season is good if the weather's right. We have a late rut like in Texas, but our rut isn't as late as a lot of places in Alabama.

How much does weather influence the hunting success in your area?

Chris Pevey: It has everything to do with it. I'd say 90 percent of your success is going to be when you've got a good, cool, crisp morning and it's the right time of the season. The woods just come alive. If you've got a full moon and it's hot, you can try your heart out and not have much success. Anything can happen, as you know, but you want both the weather and the moon phase on your side.

Charles Ruth: A tremendous amount, and this year is a good example. Up until the middle of November, we had above-average daytime temperatures, and when it's 80 degrees, it shuts the deer down completely, even during the breeding season.

The author's best personal Georgia buck.

The animals still breed, but they do all of it at night. When you have cool weather, the movements carry over into the daytime, and you see a lot more deer. Hot weather is the worst scenario for the deer hunter at any time during the season.

Jay Steen: Greatly. It's normal here to have lows in the thirties and highs in the fifties, and if you get hot weather it's bad. The best weather here is normal weather. Strong wind is negative, but windy conditions aren't nearly as bad as hot weather.

How much does weather/time of season influence where and how you hunt in your area?

Chris Pevey: It's everything, again. If it's a full moon, I'm going to go out during the midday period. The big buck is going to stay in the woods and feed on acorns, so you won't likely see him on a food plot. He's going to run some deer trails, maybe run some does if it's during the rut. I'll get on a trail or a concealed area, a little draw, and hunt tight in midday.

Charles Ruth: For me personally, if it's warm, I don't go. But for a guide with clients to put on deer, there are a couple of things you can do. When you have warm weather, stick to the woods rather than the food plots, because there's cool shade there.

Jay Steen: If you get hot weather, there's not a lot you can do to counter that. It just shuts them down and they don't move during the day. If it's early in the season and it's really hot and also dry, sometimes you can hunt your client in some of the low places that have some moisture, where there's an active growth of browse. It's tempting to just bring them in after a couple of hours on a really hot day, but we leave that up to the individual hunter. If the chances are decreasing as the heat builds, and they want to come in, we bring them in. Naturally, the more they're out there the better their chances, even if it is hot.

Chapter 8

HUNTING BRUSH-COUNTRY BUCKS

Describe your home guiding area for whitetails. What are some distinctions that set it apart?

David Davis: We're in central Texas on the edge of the Hill Country. It's rolling hills and oaks. The ranch where I work west of here is open mesquite country. The other ranch is in south Texas, and it's typical Southwest brush country. South Texas is my favorite hunting place, because you literally don't know what's going to step out. It could be a mountain lion, a javelina, a coyote, a bobcat, a six-foot rattlesnake, or it could be a 180-point deer. I love south Texas. One distinctive feature of this area would be lots of surprises while you're hunting.

Mike Gardner: We hunt in south Texas and northern Mexico. It's flat country, and fairly open. On most properties we average a deer to every twenty acres. It's an arid, desert-type climate. We're fortunate that our native vegetation has a very high protein content that tends to naturally grow big antlers on whitetails. If you look at the protein content of most of the forbs in our area, it ranges from 13 to 20 percent. That's part of the reason our area is so well known for quality whitetails. We also have, in both south Texas and northern Mexico, incredibly large acreages on private ranches. Our private ranches here average five thousand acres or more, so we're not in the situation where all our country has been broken up into small farms. It's still big, big acreage.

South Texas also carries a really good buck-to-doe ratio, without even manipulating the herd. I think it's about one buck for every three does on average. This produces a lot of deer in the 140-160 class. We take a few every year in the 180-class, but I tell clients that if that's what they have their heart set on they should probably look at Canada or somewhere else. If you want to go on a hunt and see a lot of deer between 140 and 160 points, that's what we have. We currently entertain about two hundred to two hundred fifty deer hunters per year.

The acreage on which we hunt varies from year to year, depending on rainfall and on the different types of lease agreements we negotiate. On average you'll find us hunting about 100,000 or 150,000 acres per year in Mexico, and about 50,000 acres a year in south Texas. Most of our hunting area is open, free-range country, which presents a real challenge. As for distinctions, clients tell us they've never seen bucks come to antler rattling like they do down here. It's not uncommon, in mid-December, for us to rattle up fifteen to twenty bucks from the same spot.

Don White: It's like the Golden Triangle of south Texas, and it's only three miles across the border, so it's just an extension of that Golden Triangle. The ranch is 44,000 acres, with a low fence, so the whitetails are absolutely free ranging, and we supply them no protein, no corn, nothing. We hunt them absolutely in their natural conditions. In the dozen years I've been guiding we've taken sixteen B&C deer, and numerous ones in the 160s. How many big deer we take is contingent on ranch conditions that year. It's basically flat with some small hills. It's a full-time working cattle ranch, most of which is done on horseback. There are just vast areas that don't get any pressure at all.

I've always felt that more deer die of old age on our ranch than are killed by hunters. What it takes is a large tract of land and the high-protein brush for which we're so famous. Most of the brush is less than five or six feet tall, so the deer have easy access to it. If you combine that kind of high-protein brush with a good year of rain like we're having this year, that's the key. Some of our natural foods are about 22 percent protein, which is higher than alfalfa. The very dense high-protein brush would be one distinctive feature of the ranch. Additionally, there's lots of water available year round since it's a working cattle ranch, and every pasture has at least two sources of water.

Deer and cattle don't really compete, because they eat different things, so if you're supplying the right things, like water

Guide Mike Gardner with a very happy client and his terrific brush-country buck. (Photo courtesy of Mike Gardner)

for cows, then all the wildlife benefits. On top of all that, we have fantastic genetics. If you want a wide rack, you should know that we killed two that were over twenty-seven inches wide last year, and two over twenty-eight the year before. If you want a tall rack, one of our trophy-book deer three years ago had four tines over fourteen inches. We've got kicker points, split brow tines, drop tines—a real variety of genetics.

Why should a hunter hire a guide, as opposed to being self-guided?

David Davis: The guide knows the country and the deer. He knows where to have you hunting, and he also knows what represents a respectable deer where you're hunting. You know, a guy from Florida wants to kill the first year-and-a-half-old eight-pointer he sees. I had one fellow from Florida tell me that if he'd seen that same deer in Florida, he'd have gone home and taken a week of vacation to try and kill it. Somebody's got to know what's available, and give you some guidance as to what's a trophy in that area.

Mike Gardner: For us, particularly on a paid hunt, it's very important to have competent help in field-judging the antlers. A 160-class deer is going to look so much different in other places, whether it's Canada or Georgia, than it does here. The body sizes are different in different places, and they have other different characteristics, and your guide is familiar with these differences. You might be looking at a deer you think is a 140-class deer, and your guide may know it's a 155-to-160-class deer. When I'm hunting in other parts of the world, I want to be with a guide who can tell me what a good animal looks like in that area.

Don White: I've pre-scouted and I have the tripods set up and ready to go. I scout from a distance with a spotting scope, and when I find an acceptable deer, I put in the tripod and just let it sit. I try to size up the hunters and their abilities, and when I think I've got the right hunter for the right deer, I sneak back in there and put him on the tripod one-on-one with the guide, unless I think he's very capable and able to judge deer. We don't want any mistakes, because there are a lot of young three- to four-year-old deer that we don't want to hunt, and we wouldn't put someone out alone who couldn't judge the animals well. We'll describe the deer he's hunting the best we can, and hopefully we'll even have a photo so the hunter will have an idea what he's hunting. Some 80 percent of our guys do it by themselves, and there's a lot of satisfaction in that. But they have to have an outfitter in Mexico to handle the paperwork and get them and their firearms into the country.

What is your success rate on trophy animals?

David Davis: I'd call it about 90 percent on actual kills. It's higher than that on opportunities. There are very few times we go that I can't show you a mature whitetail. I can't remember the last time that happened.

Mike Gardner: It's about 95 to 98 percent.

Don White: Nearly 100 percent. One guy went home a couple of years ago without a deer because he was holding out

Guide David Davis with a "cull buck" taken with a falling-block rifle. (Photo courtesy of David Davis)

for a 160 or better. Everybody will get an opportunity at a mature buck, and we average in the 150s.

Describe your usual hunting method and any common variations.

David Davis: We hunt food plots early and late. If the rut is on, depending on what part of the rut we're in, we walk and rattle in the middle of the day. It's pretty important to do it with as little movement as possible, because the less you move the lower your chances of getting caught by a buck. I don't jump around and kick bushes and scrape trees. We do it a minimum of twenty minutes or so in one spot before we move. It's very important, if you're rattling, to be able to see downwind a minimum of sixty to a hundred yards, because no matter where the buck starts out he's going to end up downwind. If it's hot and dry, we set up on a water hole late in the day, because it's much better to be there than on a food plot.

Mike Gardner: Most of our hunting is done in the brush country, so we have stands set up that overlook cactus flats or oak fields. In the really thick brush, roads have been cut through so the stands overlook them. The deer will cross those roads, and they'll stop in them momentarily and give us a chance. We do a lot of spot-and-stalk in the cactus flats, too, where we glass those flats and pick out a shooter deer and then go after him. We do a lot of rattling during the rut.

Don White: I usually have three guys staked out at one time per guide, taking with us the hunter we think needs help the most. We can then take input from all the guys who are out, asking what they're seeing, how many does, how did they come in, where did they come from. The guide will make an adjustment depending on how it goes, because we'll have another tripod set up either for that deer or for another that's promising. Sometimes it happens the morning of the first day. Sometimes it's the fifth day and the last hour. If the guy's capable, I'd rather that he try it on his own, because there's so much more satisfaction in that. If not, we'll stay with him.

We have a lot of roads cut through the brush with a bulldozer, long straight lines we call *senderos*. One technique we use to improve the browse is to stretch a chain between bulldozers and let them move parallel with one another, and knock down a lot of the larger brush, kind of like plowing it, because it causes a regeneration of new plant life lower to the ground and more accessible to the deer. That's also the stage when it's very nutritious, so we hunt those knockdown areas. When we find a deer that needs to be hunted, we move in there when the deer's gone, try to find a good location for the tripod, set it up and make sure visibility is good, and then we put a hunter in there when it's time.

A huge Mexico buck taken at Rancho San Enrique. (Photo courtesy of Don White)

Do you use any special techniques such as rattling, grunting, or a doe-in-heat lure?

David Davis: Rattling is my main deal, following the technique I covered before. I'm not big on cover scents, but doe-in-heat lure is more of an attractant, and it can be effective, though I seldom use it.

Mike Gardner: Obviously we use lots of rattling. We have certainly found grunt tubes to be effective. We just haven't had to use any of the chemical methods. I'm not saying I don't think it works, but in all honesty, during the rut here you feel like you could rattle two sticks together and they'd come in. When they're hot, they're hot.

Don White: We rattle and grunt a lot during the preseason to locate deer. I've had some bad experiences with hunters rattling, because you've got to make a real quick decision when the deer comes in ready for a fight, and it's hard to make a judgment. I've gotten away from rattling for clients, so I usually don't do it in a hunting situation, just because it's so easy to make a mistake. So basically it's a technique I use to get a look at the deer and cover some country to find what I need to find. A lot of times we get a photo of the deer when he comes in while we're doing this kind of scouting.

How do you hunt differently with a client/hunter, as opposed to when hunting alone?

Davis Davis: It depends on the hunter. If he can sit still, I'll hunt him just as I hunt myself. We'll get somewhere and just sit. If he's a wiggler, I have to handle it a little differently. When I hunt for myself, I do a lot of long-range hunting, so I get somewhere I can see a lot of country. With a guided hunter, I don't want him to see a deer three to four hundred yards away, because he's going to want to shoot at it, so I'm going to keep him in a lower-visibility area. We don't set our blinds up so a guy is tempted to take such long shots, because if he knocks a leg out from under that deer, it's a dead deer, especially in coyote country like ours.

Mike Gardner: When I hunt alone, I like to keep moving from location to location. When it's just me, I like to move and set up frequently and do a lot of walking and rattling. When it's one man instead of two, it's easier to hide because you make less noise. When I hunt by myself, I like to hunt a specific buck that I've targeted. To me there's nothing more fun than having a big deer that you've located, then spending quite a few days trying to pattern him, figure him out, and then get him. That's a little bit easier to do when you're by yourself. When I'm with a client, I want to show him a lot of different bucks. When I'm hunting by myself and I'm after a specific buck, I may be hunting him in an area where I know that when I go out I may not even see a buck. But since he's in that area, I may not see a lot of deer but I've got a chance of coming across him.

Don White: I do it pretty much as I've described. I've let a couple of monsters go just because I want them to stay there and breed. I haven't shot a deer personally in five years, other than management deer. I just like for my clients to shoot the kind of deer I want to shoot. A picture to me means just as much. If I can get their picture, it means I could have shot them, and there's a lot of satisfaction in showing a hunter that photograph and letting him get excited, and ultimately letting him wind up taking the deer. I have to say, though, that there's this one deer that I'd take if I could find him again! But he's crafty!

What time of the season offers the best hunting in your area [and the highest possibility of success on trophy animals]?

David Davis: The rut is best. November 15 is wide-open rut in central Texas. It may not be the very best time to rattle a deer in, but that's when the rut is most active there. In south Texas, it's December 19, give or take a day or so.

Mike Gardner: December and January. The pre-rut starts about the first of December, and it peaks around Christmas. Bucks are still coming vigorously to antler-rattling almost to mid-January.

This very large buck was taken at Rancho San Enrique, Mexico. (Photo courtesy of Don White)

Don White: Pre-rut, rut, and post-rut all pose unique challenges. Obviously, the rut is your best opportunity, so that's the best possibility of success. Personally, for me, though, I like to hunt the post-rut. There's a lot of breakage of antlers on the ranch because our buck-to-doe ratio is about 1.2:1. There's a lot of fighting, and you can think everything is broken and destroyed, then all of a sudden a magnificent deer walks out, and nobody's been fighting with him because he's the dominant buck. One of the book deer we took two years ago was like that, a 186 typical taken the last week of the season in January, and he didn't have a scratch on him. So for the really, really monster deer I'll take post-rut. Pre-rut is great, too, because the deer are just dumber than a stump, and you can pattern them and they'll do the same thing every day. When the rut starts, all bets are off. I can find you a deer in November and early December, but around Christmas when the rut hits, I can't guarantee you that he's even in the county.

How much does weather influence the hunting success in your area?

David Davis: If you asked me to draw you out the absolutely perfect scenario for a day to hunt, considering moon phase, weather conditions, overcast, temperature, wind, sunshine, etc., what would I want? I'd say none of the above. I'd answer that I'll take the rut. If it's hot they're going to rut primarily at night, so you're limited to the first hour of the morning and the last hour of the evening. The ideal condition is wide-open rut, 45 to 50 degrees Fahrenheit, and overcast. But just give me the rut, and I can work around the other factors.

Mike Gardner: Weather is a big factor. South Texas has a mild climate, and it's usually pretty warm. We like it to be cold and overcast to help kick off our rut. If we get a cold front here and the temperature drops into the 30s and 40s, it just turns our deer on in terms of rutting. When it begins to approach 70 degrees, you can just see the rut darn near shut down. When the wind picks up and we get some cold weather, boom, it turns right back on again.

Don White: The weather somewhat influences things. It can be too hot or too cold. It's a desert where we hunt, and I've seen it too cold for our deer. If it gets down below freezing, they don't move. Again, if it's up in the 80s, they lock down, too. Absolutely the best is in the 50s with some drizzle, and then you can hunt all day.

How much does weather/time of season influence where and how you hunt in your area?

David Davis: If it's hot, late in the evening I'll spend more time around water than I will around feed, whether it's a food plot or whatever. If it's bitter cold in our country, 15 degrees or so with a hard north wind, I'll set up so I can see the south slopes of a hill, preferably with gravel on it. The south slopes catch the early morning sun, and the gravel radiates that heat, and those deer go to such places like it's an electric blanket. Adverse weather certainly affects where and how I hunt, whether it's too hot or too cold.

Mike Gardner: When it's warm here, we're pretty much limited to sunup to 9:00 A.M., because the deer just don't move in the middle of the day when it's hot. The hunters can come in and watch a football game or something, or we'll go fishing or calling coyotes. We go back out about 4:30 P.M. If we get a good cold front moving in here, we'll stay out and hunt all day, particularly during the rut. At that time you see a lot of bucks traveling by themselves during the middle of the day.

Don White: The weather won't stop me or another determined hunter. If he's there, we're going to hunt for five days. If it gets too bad, we'll sit in the truck. If we've got a thunderstorm coming and we've got guys out on tripods and it's getting dangerous, we'll pick them up. But we're not going to the house. The bad weather will pass and we keep on hunting. As for time of season, I covered that above when we talked about the various phases of the rut. The biggest thing I'd add is that if you're in a drought situation, look for the water, because that's where the deer are going to be.

Chapter 9

HUNTING BIG-RIVER BUCKS

Describe your home guiding area for whitetails. What are some distinctions that set it apart?

Eric Albus: The Milk River flows out of Glacier National Park and goes north into Alberta before returning to Montana, where it flows into the Missouri River. What you see on Bill Jordan's RealTree Outdoors program is pretty much what you get here. We hunt in narrow corridors of brush adjacent to the Milk River, and the edges of alfalfa and barley fields. It's unique in that most of our bends of brush are less than fifteen acres in size, some of them as small as five to six acres. In those brushy areas there can be anywhere from twenty to a hundred and fifty head of deer in each patch. You're going to see a lot of deer every day, even on a bad day. Some distinctions of the area are related to this unique kind of terrain. In a five-day hunt, you've got pretty much a sure bet that you're going to see a Pope and Young deer, because we have a lot of 130-to-150-class bucks. Last year my bow hunters were over 100 percent on legitimate shots at trophy deer, and the shots averaged twenty yards. A couple of guys missed two or three times.

Keaton Kelso: My Kansas ground is very open, with some square-mile sections being completely in agricultural fields. They grow primarily winter wheat here, some corn, and a lot of alfalfa. Some of the alfalfa fields are four to five hundred acres, and these are a big attraction for deer in these parts. There are a lot of thick, brushy draws in between those fields, and that's pretty much what we hunt. Many people come to Kansas expecting heavy hardwoods, but if I have just fifteen acres of timber, that's a big patch. Conservation Reserve Program (CRP) patches are another good place to hunt in

Guide James Woodley's pair of Illinois bucks died fighting during the rut, not as a result of hunting activity. (Photo courtesy of James Woodley)

our part of the state. If you find sixty to eighty acres of CRP land, you're bound to have good deer there. Mature bucks especially like to bed down in that overgrown CRP land, so they can see all around. Does and small bucks bed mostly in the brush and timber.

Kansas is a draw state, but we have a transferable landowner system, too. Landowners have to put in for a draw, and if they're drawn they can transfer their tags to a nonresident. That tag is good for the whole county the landowner lives in, not just on his land. Missouri sells over-the-counter deer tags. There's some cropland there with rivers and creeks running through it, but there's a lot of heavy timber, too, so it's totally different hunting. Another different type of country is a broad strip of sand dunes that runs the length of the state, which looks a lot like Texas brush country. It's highly productive for whitetails because there's little hunting pressure, and we take some terrific bucks there. The distinctive feature in Kansas is the sheer length of the shots you sometimes have to take because of the wide-open nature of the country. In Missouri it's much closer and much different, since you're on a stand hunting hardwood bottoms most of the time.

James Woodley: We're in the classic Midwest, located in what's called our Golden Triangle, which consists of Pike, Brown, and Adams counties. Pike and Adams are usually first and second for record book animals every year, and Brown is right there with them. The area where we operate is split about 60-40 between timbered ground and farmland. There are a lot of big fields of corn, soybeans, and alfalfa, along with a lot of edges. It's perfect deer habitat. We have about eight thousand acres on which we hunt. The thing that makes it different from other places is our longtime management program. One of the big things we do is harvest more does than we do bucks, trying to keep the herd in check. Something we do to encourage people to harvest does is that when someone takes a mature doe, we put his name in a hat, and at the end of the season we draw one name and give that person a free hunt.

Why should a hunter hire a guide, as opposed to being self-guided?

Eric Albus: If you're after a better-than-average animal, finding a property to hunt that animal without the help of a quality outfitter has become increasingly difficult, to the point where it's highly unlikely. You need to hire a qualified professional to help you. Time is a precious commodity these days, so saving time is a main objective. Finding the right property, getting permission to hunt, scouting, and doing all the other necessary preliminaries are greatly facilitated by hiring a quality outfitter. Hiring such a person is a time-management tool, and it makes good sense.

Keaton Kelso: Well, I'm not opposed to being self-guided, and I do it for myself whenever possible. But if I had one vacation and I wanted to kill a big deer, I'd get a guide. Your odds of taking a real trophy are dramatically increased when you're on a guided hunt. I love a self-guided situation, but if I'm looking for something special, the guide knows the best places and the best possibilities. If you have the time, self-guiding is a good option, but if you're on a fixed time schedule, a guide is the way to go. The things you get from a guide are numerous—stands are up, food plots are planted, feeders are running, trails are cut, and so on. If you're self-guided, you have none of this in place.

James Woodley: I think it kind of depends on the person, but I'd say that most people don't have the time to spend to find a trophy animal, nor the knowledge to set up a good situation for hunting. A lot of people have only a few days to hunt nowadays. When they come here, everything is ready for them, and hopefully we have an idea where the deer are going to be.

Guide Keaton Kelso is proud of his personal Kansas trophy buck. (Photo courtesy of Keaton Kelso)

What is your success rate on trophy animals?

Eric Albus: The last five years we've averaged 132 Pope and Young gross on our archery hunts, with 75 to 85 percent of our hunters getting shots, and about 65 percent scoring a kill. Our gun hunters have been 100 percent on kills for the past five years, with an average Boone and Crockett gross score of 143.

Keaton Kelso: We're about 25 percent on 150-class animals or better. A 150-class buck is a trophy animal, in my estimation. Typically, if four people come, one person will go home without a buck, one will take one that's 150 or better, and two will go home with a buck that's in the 120-to-150 range. My advice to clients is that if the buck is the biggest they've ever seen, and they'd be happy with that buck, shoot it! Then do your part and be happy with that buck, regardless of what it scores. Last year we had a guy take a giant old deer with 6½-inch bases, and it was so old that it was on the downswing as far as antlers go. It had short tines but was massively heavy all the way to the tips. Still, I knew it wouldn't score well because it didn't have the length to go with the mass. The hunter was tickled to death while the buck was on the ground, high-fiving and dancing around. He was the same way back in camp, happy telling the story and happy with the successful hunt. Then he wanted me to take a tape measure to his buck. I told him, I'm sorry, I don't want to score your buck. I didn't want to take the trophy out of that great buck just because of what it would score on a tape measure.

James Woodley: Last year opportunity at a trophy buck was 65 percent, and the kill rate was 24 percent. That's pretty typical. In the opportunity category we include deer that people passed up that were trophy class but not what they wanted. The 65 percent also includes deer that were shot at and missed, or wounded and lost.

Describe your usual hunting method and any common variations.

Eric Albus: Generally we do all our hunting from ladder stands that are about fifteen feet high. On occasion we use a pop-up

Some monster bucks come out of Kansas and Missouri's big-river country each year. (Photo courtesy of Keaton Kelso)

blind or a ground blind, because sometimes we hunt in areas where we don't have any trees. Our trees here at Milk River aren't very big, anyway. All our hunts are in the afternoon, and we have them on the stand from 2:00 P.M. until dark. We do occasionally use spot-and-stalk on a gun hunt, using available cover to get within range of a buck, but it's tough because there are so many deer and so many pairs of eyes watching you.

Keaton Kelso: We live and die by www.terraserver.com. On their aerial photos we find the funnels between feeding and bedding areas. We set up our tree stands in those funnels. We put a tree stand closer to the bedding area early in the season, and closer to the food plot later in the season. Then we spend hours and hours glassing our areas. If a guy is going unguided, he'd be better off leaving his rifle in the truck the first three days and just glass, glass, glass. Too often hunters pile off into the timber without any idea of what they're doing. They need to know what's there and how it's moving, but instead they get in there and stir up their deer. We get in and set up on the funnels, using that Terraserver map to set things up, and then we do a lot of glassing.

James Woodley: Our usual method is hunting from tree stands. Every morning before we take the hunters out, the guides get together, look at our aerial photos, and check the wind. For us, the wind is the most critical factor in choosing which stand to hunt from. We put out around two hundred tree stands a year; the idea is to have stands set for every possible wind direction. It seems there is always some wind that leaves us with not enough stands to hunt, but usually it works out. We also check it in the afternoon before putting them out, because if the wind's not right for a stand, they're not going to hunt it and risk blowing that deer out of there.

If we have to, we'll move and hang a stand on the other side of the field or draw. These are all portable stands, mostly API Baby Grand stands, and we reach them with climbing sticks or ladders or whatever the hunter is comfortable using. Some guys don't like the heights, so most of our stands are set to hit a happy medium—high enough for everybody who wants to be high, but low enough that others don't get too nervous. Most of them are set at sixteen to twenty feet up.

Do you use any special techniques such as rattling, grunting, or a doe-in-heat lure?

Eric Albus: We've had excellent success with all these special techniques, as well as with decoys, especially during the pre-rut and post-rut periods. What it takes is a good buck population.

Keaton Kelso: We use pretty much everything during certain times of the year. We use a lot of grunting and rattling during bow season, because that's the rut. During rifle season, we don't do very much of that, because rifle season is post-rut. I do occasionally use a doe bleat during the post-rut, and sometimes I pull in nice bucks that way. We make use of decoys during archery season. We killed a good buck just last year using a decoy, and he came in to about ten yards, getting ready to put a thumping on that decoy. We also use scents and fake scrapes and that kind of thing. All these techniques make your percentages go up.

James Woodley: We use such techniques, especially during the pre-rut period at the end of October. Rattling works really well then, though it kind of depends on the year and what the weather's doing. We also have really good success with a doe-in-heat lure and some of the bleat calls. I recommend that if you're going to use these special techniques, do it full bore, or else leave it alone. Don't use them as a last-ditch effort to get a deer.

How do you hunt differently with a client/hunter, as opposed to when hunting alone?

Eric Albus: I really don't do anything different. I hunt exactly the same way and in the same places as I do with clients.

An outstanding Montana buck taken with guide Eric Albus. (Photo courtesy of Eric Albus)

Keaton Kelso: If I have a truly good hunter with a high experience level, I'll get him right in there with the deer and hunt like I do by myself. If my hunter is inexperienced, I'll keep him out of that close contact and we'll hunt from a distance, out about two hundred yards or so from where I expect the deer to be, the ditch bottoms and bedding and feeding areas. We do a lot of watching and glassing. I like to get in close personally, and I hunt a lot with my rifle from bow stands. I'm a firm believer that those big, mature bucks are not going to come out on those food plots during daylight hours. They're down in that brush, and they'll wait it out until you can't see them in your scope before they get up.

James Woodley: One of the main things I do when I hunt by myself is that I get a little bit higher than average, if possible. The higher you can get, the better for bowhunting, to minimize the effect of wind. All the rest I do exactly the same.

What time of the season offers the best hunting in your area [and the highest possibility of success on trophy animals]?

Eric Albus: Like anywhere, the rut is probably best. It begins around the tenth of November. We've also taken some really big deer in September. Our archery season starts the first Saturday in September and runs to mid-October, and our gun season starts in late October and runs until just after Thanksgiving. We have a long season, and we've taken good bucks at all times during the season.

Keaton Kelso: If a guy is a gun hunter, I like the early muzzleloader season. You have a good chance of not shooting anything, but your chance at a trophy animal is higher. During rifle season, we kill some very good bucks, but it's not easy to pattern them. In Kansas, the bow season is the time to see lots of unbelievable bucks. It's the peak of the rut, and you'll see six to eight bucks a day, and most of them will be Pope and Young. In Missouri, the rifle hunt is during the rut, so that's a really good time and place to take a great deer, too.

James Woodley: The peak of the rut is the tenth of November, so the first two weeks of November are best.

A great Illinois buck taken with Heartland Outfitters. (Photo courtesy of James Woodley)

How much does weather influence the hunting success in your area?

Eric Albus: The weather plays a role on any hunt almost anywhere, and here is no exception. However, I do feel that the weather is less of a factor here than in most other places. We normally have so many deer that even during a few days of bad weather our hunters are seeing good numbers of deer. That's not to say that when the weather turns better the hunting isn't better, because it definitely is.

Keaton Kelso: That's part of the crapshoot when you come as a client. It's one thing I can't control. Weather plays a huge role in our early muzzleloader season, when we could have a heat wave and 100-degree temperatures during the day, and you just won't see any deer. If it's cool, say 70 degrees during the day, deer just appear everywhere. During rifle season this year, we had a mediocre first week. The second week, a huge cold front pushed through, and we had ten inches of snow. We had about 50 percent of our clients shoot 150s or better that week. It's a temperature issue. If it's cold and crisp, it's really good. I think weather is a big influence in almost all kinds of hunting.

James Woodley: Weather can be a really big factor for the hunter, because a couple of days of bad weather can cut badly into your hunting time. We've had some years when it was 80 degrees the second week of November. The bucks are really fat just before the rut and field dress from 180 to 200 pounds. If it gets hot at all, they're going to do all their rutting at night.

How much does weather/time of season influence where and how you hunt in your area?

Eric Albus: Not very much at all. We hunt in the same areas all season, no matter what the weather. We may change tactics a little depending on the weather and time of season, like using some of the special techniques when the situation is right, but that's about all we ever change.

Massive antlers characterize this awesome Kansas buck. (Photo courtesy of Keaton Kelso)

Keaton Kelso: It depends more on your crops. Early in the season the winter wheat isn't up, but by December it's growing, and the deer will be feeding in those fields. When it's bitter cold, I've seen them walk right across an open alfalfa field and go into a milo field and start eating. They really hit our milo fields and cornfields. As the weather gets colder, they're going to be using different food sources, and we have to account for that in our strategy. Also, when it's cold, they're going to feed more, and you need to stay in that stand longer because those bucks are not going to be able to just go somewhere and lie down all day. They get up and go feed, so with colder weather you get more movement from the deer.

James Woodley: Early in the season, the kinds of food available to the deer can be a big factor. We're mainly hunting food sources, and early in the season the acorns start dropping about the time the soybeans turn yellow. The deer don't like soybean foliage when it's starting to turn yellow, so at that time they switch to feeding on acorns. About the only field source of deer forage at that time is green alfalfa fields, because neither soybeans nor corn are ready. Give it a month, and the corn and beans are both all mature and dry; when the weather starts getting cold, the deer start hitting the corn and beans. Deer are easier to hunt when it's cold because they move around more. How much we move our hunters around depends on all these factors.

Chapter 10
HUNTING COLD-COUNTRY BUCKS

Describe your home guiding area for whitetails. What are some distinctions that set it apart?

Gary Drinkall: We're located south and west of Dawson Creek, and my area goes all the way to the Alberta border. It's all hay and alfalfa fields with lots of bush around them. There are plenty of creek bottoms, mountains, hills, and so on. It's a lot different from the big Alberta country. It's more a Western kind of cattle country, with lots of rivers and mountains. Alberta has big, vast fields, and we're distinctive in that this British Columbia country has more secluded little hayfields up in small valleys. There are large sections of bush with little alfalfa fields on the back of them.

It's big country, but it's not big farming country like Alberta, and there's very little grain farming here. That being the case, what we do is put in ten-acre food plots in strategic places. We plant peas, fall rye, and barley, which is a little different than in other parts of the world because here we can grow these with no problem. Our food plots offer a variety of food for the deer to eat, so they're effective, which is nice for us. You go into a ten-square-mile area and stick in a ten-acre food plot, and soon you've got every deer in that area coming to it.

I always include the fall rye because it grows four or five inches tall and then stays green, even if we've got a foot of snow on top of it. Those deer will pick at it all winter, and it's the first thing available in the spring. That rye goes crazy when the weather starts warming, and it gives our deer the chance to put on some fast weight gain early, after the long, hard winter.

Rene Semple: We're seventy-five miles northwest of Edmonton, Alberta. It's rolling parkland, rolling hills with deciduous trees such as poplar and willow, with a lot of river and creek drainages running through it. We don't have a lot of big timber in this area. We have mixed cattle ranching with grain fields, and some alfalfa fields and row-crop farming. It's got everything, and the whitetails really like it. One main distinction is that we hunt predominantly private ground instead of public land. All our guides are local guys, and we know a lot of the ranchers; we get along really well with them, and they let us hunt.

Jim Shockey: I have eight hundred square miles of territory in Saskatchewan that is my exclusive guiding area. Saskatchewan is my home province in Canada and I grew up there, so my relatives all still live there, and I've been hunting whitetails there for over thirty years. There isn't a fence or farm anywhere in my guiding area, so it's unique in that it's pure wilderness white-tailed deer hunting. The distinctive feature is the size of the white-tailed deer here. Saskatchewan has become the mecca of whitetail hunting. If you want a big whitetail, go to Saskatchewan, because the odds of getting such a deer are higher here than anywhere else in North America.

Why should a hunter hire a guide, as opposed to being self-guided?

Gary Drinkall: If you've got a good guide or outfitter, he's going to have good property, and he's worked his butt off to get that property. A hunter is going to increase his odds dramatically by hunting the very best country available. As an outfitter, I'm not generally going to put in a food plot and a stand on a piece of land that doesn't have any deer. I want the very best I can get. Your guide and outfitter are your connection to the prime hunting spots, and they already know where those spots are before you arrive.

Rene Semple: You need a guide in order to have access to and experience with an area. If you don't know the place you're going to hunt, it really helps to have someone with you who does. There are travel corridors that these bucks use, and we watch them change with changing conditions, hunting pressure and the like. One week there will be no deer in a given area, and a week later deer are using the area heavily. If you come into a place cold, you can't know that kind of thing. Another thing is the regulations, which vary from province to province, and a good guide will help you stay within the law.

Jim Shockey: Number one, the guide has done all the preseason scouting for you. Self-guided hunts are sometimes penny-wise and dollar-foolish. If you want to walk around and enjoy the fresh air, that's great. But if you want to get serious about getting a big deer in an allotted amount of time, then a guided hunt is by far the best way to go. Of course, not everyone can afford it; if you don't have much money to spare, a self-guided hunt will be your best bet. It's not like whitetail hunting is in any way truly dangerous, certainly not in the way of, say, mountain hunting, where you need a guide just for your own safety.

I don't have a problem with self-guided whitetail hunters, but even if they're good at it, it will take three years of hunting three or four weeks each year before they'll even begin to get comfortable in a given area. You can save those three years and those weeks each year by going on a guided hunt. Some people have plenty of time and no money, while others have money and no time, so in the final analysis it's a function of your socioeconomic status, I'd say.

What is your success rate on trophy animals?

Gary Drinkall: I think we were twelve for fifteen last season, and all of them were mature bucks.

Rene Semple: On opportunity at a mature buck, it must be around 90 percent, and it's been pretty steady there. A mature Alberta whitetail is a 140-to-145-inch deer, and don't let anybody tell you differently. They're not all 170 B&C deer, even when they're in their prime at five or six years old. On actual kills on big deer, our rate is about 70 percent. Some of our bucks make B&C every year.

Jim Shockey: I'd say all of my clients will see at least one buck that scores between 130 and 150 B&C points. Some of my clients will see ten different deer in that range. That said, those aren't bucks that we're trying to kill. We're hunting for bucks that will score over 150, and we're somewhere in the 50 percent range for bucks that score that well. It would be a lot higher if guys would know what they're looking at, and hit what they're shooting at, and not shoot something smaller before the big one walks in. These are very important factors in the success rate. There's almost no hunter who is ever completely satisfied with the animal he takes. Frequently I hear, "If it didn't have this sticker point, or if this tine was a little bit longer, or if it was one inch wider..." Well, if it had stripes on it, it'd be something different altogether, too.

Describe your usual hunting method and any common variations.

Gary Drinkall: It's over food plots and baits. A lot of stands are back off alfalfa fields, or the food plot is on a fence line, so I can keep my hunter back in the bush but he can still see a good part of the field. These big whitetails, even where it's secluded, are like ghosts when they get to be four to five years old. Tucking the hunter back in the bush a little way helps us to see and kill some of the older bucks. We check the wind when we get up for breakfast, and then by daylight we're in a stand facing the wind. Another guide or I will come back to check on the hunter in late morning, and then the hunter stays in the stand until dark.

I really like the hunters to be on the stand in the middle of the day because that's when the mature bucks are traveling. The whole key to killing a big whitetail is not letting him know he's being hunted, and there are several steps to coming up with a good plan. The first one is figuring out where he is, and then scouting, scouting, and doing some more scouting. We're out there 365 days a year, looking for rubs, scrapes, track size, sheds, and a visual on the animal if possible. A big white-tailed buck will only move in deep brush during the day, and then sneak out onto the food plots at night to eat. You just know a good location, because not only does it have signs of big buck activity, but it also has a certain feel to it that experience will confirm for you.

Once I've found a magic spot, we examine it with a fine-tooth comb to determine the best spot to place a stand, which, I hope, will be between the feeding and bedding areas. It has to be a spot you can move into and out of like a ghost so that the buck never knows you're there. Both your trail and the stand have to be located where the buck is least likely to show up and discover your scent. You want the deer out in front of you and the wind in your face, and you're all set. Wind is the number one factor, because if it's wrong you simply don't have a chance. Even if a doe catches your scent and blows, the game is over. That monster buck is most likely just lying back in the brush listening for signs of danger, and almost anything out of order will cause him to lie low. Once you, the hunter, are on that stand without alarming any deer, just sit back and patiently enjoy it. If you put your time in, eventually a shooter is going to show up in front of you.

Rene Semple: Usually we take the hunters to the stand in the dark, but in some areas we want to wait until daylight to position them. There are some stretches of open ground where you want to be able to see deer as you go in, and you'll miss them if you do that in the dark. We've taken quite a few deer on the way to the stand. When the hunters are put into the blind, for safety purposes they're in radio contact with their guide all the time. It also enables them to call us if they get a deer. The guide doesn't come back to camp when he puts his hunter in the blind, but he goes out scouting, looking for hot sign, and so on. Because of pressure, the deer change their habits sometimes, and if an area goes cold, we can move the hunter to a place where there is more sign.

All our blinds are portable, so we're always moving stuff around. You'd think that our movement would affect the deer, but it rarely does. Guys on tree stands seem to affect deer more than people in blinds do. We're more into hunting in travel corridors than on scrape lines because by the time the rut gets rolling, bucks are on the move too much to work scrapes. We've had new scrape lines open up, hunted them hard, and never saw the buck.

Jim Shockey: Our standard method is stand hunting. Our hunters sit on their stands from dawn until dark without moving. We are allowed to bait in our areas, but we set up the stands in the best areas, and not always over bait. We use pop-up tent blinds so that we can move them, and we hunt in crossing areas, on scrape lines, and so forth.

Judd Moritz with a great Saskatchewan buck he took with guide Jim Shockey. (Photo courtesy of Jim Shockey)

Do you use any special techniques such as rattling, grunting, or a doe-in-heat lure?

Gary Drinkall: We sometimes hunt on scrape lines in really thick brush by rattling and grunting, especially if the hunter wants to get out of the stand for a while during midday. It's got to be a calm day and a hot scrape line, or it doesn't work. We set up in thick stuff downwind of a scrape line. We usually put a little of that doe-in-heat stuff on the bottom of our pants legs, too, as a cover scent more than anything. I've never had a really huge buck come in doing that, but we've killed some 150-point bucks that way.

Rene Semple: I've used all these methods with some success, though rattling doesn't work really well up here because of our low deer density. Special techniques like those probably work to some degree, but in our area success mainly comes from getting in those travel corridors and putting in your time on the stand. Grunting works pretty well, and we use the grunt tube quite a bit.

Jim Shockey: No, we stay away from such techniques, because most people are incapable of using them properly anyway. What you're really doing in most cases is alerting the buck to your exact location. Those types of tactics can work well, and I'm not saying they don't, but they work best when you're mobile. When you're stationary, you're only going to give away your location.

How do you hunt differently with a client/hunter, as opposed to when hunting alone?

Gary Drinkall: When I hunt by myself I do a lot of still-hunting. If we get two or three inches of fresh snow, and I can cut a fresh buck track crossing the road, I'll just jump out and head right after him. I've tried it with clients, but two people pushing through the bush just isn't going to work. The hunter has to be a good snapshooter, and for your client you're trying to get a rough estimate of what the deer is going to score. You

An Alberta buck to make one proud, taken with Rene and Kelly Semple. (Photo courtesy of Rene Semple)

just don't have time to do that when you're still-hunting after a whitetail. But I love it because it teaches you how that deer moves, especially when he's rutting. It's great to follow as he circles back on you and shows you all his moves.

Rene Semple: I really don't do anything differently. You have to take into consideration the hunter's physical condition and abilities, and hunt according to his pace. Other than that, you're not going to change very much in the way you hunt for yourself.

Jim Shockey: Again, that's a two-sided question for me, because when I hunt alone, with no cameraman with me, I'll use a combination of techniques. I'll track, I'll rattle, I'll stand hunt, I'll still-hunt, I'll spot and stalk. I determine what I'm going to do during a given day depending on weather conditions, ground conditions, the sign I'm seeing, where I'm hunting, how much terrain I'm hunting, and so on. Then it's pretty easy to kill any whitetail I go after because up in our country we don't have fences to tell me I can't go there. If I get on a buck's track, I'll kill that deer eventually. But with a camera along, I hunt exactly the same way our clients do, sitting from dawn to dark. If there's any difference, it's that I hunt five weeks every fall, instead of being locked into a one-week guided hunt.

What time of the season offers the best hunting in your area (and the highest possibility of success on trophy animals)?

Gary Drinkall: Everybody wants to hunt the rut, of course. I personally like the first ten days of November. Here in British Columbia we've only got twenty days, 1 November through 20 November, so we run two ten-day hunts. We generally kill our biggest bucks on the first hunt. They come into the baits and claim them like a grizzly, and if any younger bucks come around they run them off. As soon as they start rutting they start traveling, and they can be harder to hunt. When they're pre-rut, they often won't leave. We had a lady last year miss a buck, then the next day she saw him again and shot him in the leg. Later that same day, he came back in and she killed him! That was his bait, and nothing was going to run him off!

Rene Semple: I'd say all of November, but especially the last three weeks.

Jim Shockey: It's definitely the late season, all through November and the first part of December, which includes the middle of the rut.

How much does weather influence the hunting success in your area?

Gary Drinkall: The weather is a factor, big time. In Canada we've got to have cold weather to keep the does moving. If you keep the does moving, you keep the bucks moving, especially in a food-plot scenario like we have. Cold weather really increases your odds because the deer are going to be up and around more often during daylight. Last year everything was going so well on the first hunt because the weather was cold, and I was looking forward to the second hunt. Boom, we got hit with a chinook (warm, westerly winds), and that was it. We finally got into some deer the last few days, but for seven or eight days the wind blew about 60 miles an hour and it warmed up to 60 degrees. Warm weather combined with lack of snow is devastating.

Rene Semple: Weather definitely does have an impact. If it gets warm, the bucks seem to be much more nocturnal. The way it works, I think, is that the bucks are still fairly fat early in the season, they've got their winter coat on, they're all muscled up, and they're full of testosterone. They heat up easily. When it gets warm, they still breed, but they aren't nearly as active, and most activity takes place at night when it's cooler. We've shot deer in wicked snowstorms, and even in the heat, but when the weather turns warm we don't generally do as well.

Jim Shockey: Weather is the determining factor on how many deer we see and what size they are. Cold is best, warm is worst, and there are variations on both of these. Cold and windy, cold and snowy, cold and overcast, cold and still, but the bottom line in our area is that you want it cold as opposed to warm.

How much does weather/time of season influence where and how you hunt in your area?

Gary Drinkall: With the food plots, we're pretty much hunting in the same country every year. Each ranch will have one deer taken off it, and that's it for the season. The guys coming on the first hunt will be on one group of ranches, and the guys on the second hunt will hunt on different ranches. What I'm trying to do is build a pool of older bucks that have a chance to grow up. That's why I've never gone for large numbers of hunters. I didn't want the stress, and I just wanted to take a limited number of guys on my best pieces of property. We don't really change the places we hunt in response to the time of season or the weather, but weather is a huge factor in hunter success.

Rene Semple: As the season progresses, we're always changing our hunting locations for various reasons, especially signs that deer are moving in an area. We're always shifting our stands around according to conditions. When we see an area go active, it's time to put a hunter in there, and usually we're successful.

Jim Shockey: There's no change in the way we hunt due to these factors. We hunt exactly the same throughout our five-week hunting season. There's no benefit to changing. The way we do it is already the best way to hunt, so why fix something that's not broken?

Chapter 11
HUNTING HIGH-DESERT BUCKS

Describe your home guiding area for whitetails. What are some distinctions that set it apart?

Duwane Adams: I guide throughout the state of Arizona. It's all broken down into zones and units, and I've hunted in every zone and unit in Arizona. I guide from the desert floor, some three thousand feet of elevation where there's a lot of cactus, up to six or seven thousand feet where it's thick oak country. We hunt in it all. More than anything else, the cactus plant sets it apart. The cactus is one of the deer's main items of diet, and the types and amounts they consume vary with the time of year. Most people don't know that. Deer eat the barrel cactus in December, for example, and the cholla cactus in January. So in hunting these deer, it's very important to know your cacti.

Carlos Gonzalez Hermosillo: My area in Sonora has grassy hills with forty-five-degree slopes. Most of our hunting occurs between four thousand and six thousand feet of elevation. In the bottoms of the canyons are oak trees and medium-thick brush six to twelve feet in height. The distance between one ridge crest and the next is approximately five hundred to fifteen hundred yards. It's a hunt where you go down off the edge of a canyon, and then over to the next one, and so on. Sometimes we jump the deer out of the bottoms and get a shot. The most important thing, though, is to glass well from wherever you can. The distinctive feature of our area is the conservation we have done to benefit the Coues deer. When I started our program on our best ranches, they were just like any other ranch in Mexico. There were some deer, but in a week maybe you would see only one. Fifteen years later, everybody wants to hunt on these ranches because you see fifteen to twenty bucks a day. Conservation is the big difference.

Client Craig Hayward's Arizona Coues deer, taken on public land with guide Duwane Adams. (Photo courtesy of Duwane Adams)

Kirk Kelso: The areas where we hunt are in southern Arizona and northern Sonora, and you really can't tell the terrain in one place from the other. It's more the lower number of hunters in Sonora that sets it apart. We have under lease in Sonora some 330,000 acres of prime Coues deer country, and the deer inhabit all of it. We hunt on any public land in which a client draws a tag in Arizona, too. We hunt at elevations from about three thousand feet up to about six thousand feet, and that includes from the desert scrub/ocotillo thickets up into the oaks with grassy rolling hills. Coues deer also live down in the flat desert mule deer country and up higher in the pines. However, there are no good glassing places to help you locate them, so even though they live there you can't effectively hunt them. We focus on the areas where we can be successful, and those are the areas where we can get vantage points and glass.

Why should a hunter hire a guide, as opposed to being self-guided?

Duwane Adams: I ask clients what they do for a living. A client may say, "I'm an engineer for General Electric," or something. I remind him that if I went to his office and tried to tell him how to run it, he'd throw me out of there. And hunters admit that's true. So I tell them, well, you just got into my office. Hunting today is so expensive, with tags, transportation, time off, and so on, that when you get out there, you'd better have somebody waiting who knows the country and the animals. By the time you've learned what you have to know, how to get there, what to do, a million things, you've run out of time and you've done nothing. I tell people that even a bad guide is better than no guide at all.

Carlos Gonzalez Hermosillo: The guide knows the country, and that's the big advantage. A hunter might know how to hunt, know how to get around in the mountains, be in good shape, and know the animals well. But you don't know the local situation like a local does, and when you're an outsider you need a guide. That goes for any hunt almost anywhere when you aren't a local.

An excellent Sonora Coues deer taken with Pusch Ridge Outfitters. (Photo courtesy of Kirk Kelso)

You are the stranger, the nonresident, and it's wise to hire the best and most knowledgeable guide you can find, and then you should have a good hunt.

Kirk Kelso: A hunter should hire a guide if he's unfamiliar with the area or unfamiliar with the habits of the animal. If he just wants to kill any animal, then maybe a guide isn't his best choice. But if he wants to take a good, respectable representative of the species, then he needs to hire someone to help him. That's especially true if he's not familiar with how to get around in the country where he's going to hunt, or if he's not familiar with the habits of the animal. Most people from back East or from the Midwest have never hunted this type of animal or in this type of terrain. It's a big advantage for them to hire a guide to show them what they need to do to be successful.

What is your success rate on trophy animals?

Duwane Adams: 100 percent. That's on opportunity, of course. I had one guy shoot 26 times last year at five different bucks! He didn't kill a deer, but that's not my fault.

Carlos Gonzalez Hermosillo: We have a very high success rate, and we don't shoot anything less than a 4X4. It's almost 100 percent for taking an animal. Over the years we've taken about fifteen hundred hunters for Coues deer, and probably five or six haven't harvested an animal. Almost all the kills were on trophy animals, too.

Kirk Kelso: Our rate runs about 120 percent, year in and year out, because we have a good number of hunters who take two deer. If you're talking about the percentage of hunters who kill an animal, it probably runs around 90 percent. If you're talking about the percentage of opportunity to kill a 100-inch Coues deer, it would be well over 100 percent. A lot of our clients have already killed 105-to-110-inch Coues deer, and now they're looking for the exceptional head and they pass up anything else. Of course, that comes out of your success rate on harvest, but the opportunity is always there on every single one of our Sonoran hunts. On the other hand, some of our clients have chosen to shoot deer that score less than that, because that's still a trophy to them.

Describe your usual hunting method and any common variations.

Duwane Adams: Glassing, glassing, and when you're tired of that, it's glassing some more. We get set up way before the sun comes up, and then we're glassing until dark. It's only glassing, because that's the only way to kill a Coues deer, seriously. When we spot a good buck, we close the distance as much as possible. A lot of times we have to wait until he gets up before we can shoot. Maybe we can see parts of him while he's resting, but when he gets up, that's when we take him.

Carlos Gonzalez Hermosillo: Basically, we have the ranch divided into several areas, and we leave the ranch by Jeep and

The author hunting in bewitching high-desert, Coues deer country.

drive to the top. We choose one canyon and start glassing from there. If the hunter is in good shape, we hunt down, which is the easiest way for the hunters, and the Jeep meets us down lower five or six hours later. We then go back to camp to rest, and we do a two-hour session in the late evening that lasts until it's too dark to see well.

Kirk Kelso: We developed our method of hunting Coues deer long ago in order to be successful at this long-range game. What we do is to locate areas on our properties where we can have large areas to glass—big canyon systems and the like. We sit on these glassing points and we'll glass for five or six hours sometimes. We try to pick out those deer bedded or moving in the bottoms, whatever we have to do. The way to tell a good Coues whitetail guide and hunter is that his boots look like they're new and the seat of his pants is worn out. That's because you have to spend the time behind the binoculars in order to be successful.

In Arizona, we get up early and climb a long way in the dark because we're hunting public land and we have to get to certain places before anyone else does. We try to be sitting where we want to be glassing by the time it's first light. In Sonora, we don't even leave camp until it's light, because there the buck of a lifetime could be a couple of hundred yards from camp, and you're going to drive right by him in the dark. It's just an entirely different situation down there.

Do you use any special techniques such as rattling, grunting, or a doe-in-heat lure?

Duwane Adams: No.

Carlos Gonzalez Hermosillo: We have tried rattling, but it doesn't work, and we know that there are many deer in the area, and they themselves rattle their antlers when they fight. But rattling doesn't work here for some reason. Our best technique is to simply know the area extremely well and use this to advantage, knowing where the deer are, knowing where the bucks are and where they aren't. Basically, our knowledge of

An unbelievable Coues buck taken in Sonora with guide Carlos Hermosillo. (Photo courtesy of Carlos Hermosillo)

the area is working better for us than any gimmick you can devise. I do use a grunt call or fawn bleat when the deer is in sight, like when they're lying down and the hunter wants them standing. A little bleat or grunt, and the deer usually will stand up but not run away. They get up because they're curious but not frightened. Sometimes you can only see the antlers above the brush, and these calls can get them up.

I let the personality of the hunter dictate what I do. When I see someone who is patient, I wait. When I see a person who's impatient, and who says after a few minutes, "Maybe we should look for another deer," I say, "Why? We've been looking all day and now we've found the deer, and you don't want it because it's behind a bush? Give me a break!" When they're that impatient I'll try the grunt call, and many times it works well.

Kirk Kelso: We don't use any of those techniques. The reason we don't is that in order to be successful at killing big trophy Coues whitetails, you have to kill them when they don't know you're there. It's really a three-step process: Spot, stalk, and snipe. If you use rattling, or a grunt call, or some kind of lure, you're doing nothing but focusing their attention directly onto you. It's also usually impossible even to get onto the same slope with a major buck without his knowing you're there, because it's very noisy walking most of the time. I use rattling horns only when a buck is bedded and we can't get a shot because he's in the brush or something of that nature, or if the rut's going on. In such a case we might rattle some just to make him stand up and move a little bit. In that situation we're already in position and we're getting ready to snipe him, but we're not able to do this because of where he's lying.

How do you hunt differently with a client/hunter, as opposed to when hunting alone?

Duwane Adams: I hunt exactly the same way. I don't change it in the least. I glass for myself, and I glass for my clients just like they're my sons.

Carlos Gonzalez Hermosillo: I don't really hunt any differently. I do exactly the same things. I go up, I use the Jeep, I work down, and so on. The only difference is that I've been fortunate to kill a lot of big Coues deer, so I'm only interested in the biggest deer. I pass up many deer that would be a dream deer to most hunters.

Kirk Kelso: It's absolutely the same. To me, as a guide, if I take a client into the field and he kills a world-record deer, that's a deer that I killed. I just didn't pull the trigger.

What time of the season offers the best hunting in your area [and the highest possibility of success on trophy animals]?

Duwane Adams: The late hunt during December.

Carlos Gonzalez Hermosillo: Traditionally, our best hunts are from 5 January until 25 January. The rut peaks about 15 January, so those two weeks are the best. On the other hand, you could say that in an area like ours where there is low hunting pressure, low impact by predators, and no poaching, the best time to hunt is simply whenever you are there.

Kirk Kelso: Arizona starts the season in October and runs into December. In Mexico they start the season in December and run into January, and actually that's the best time to hunt. That's because the rut kicks in about December and runs into January, making the hunting more productive during that time period.

How much does weather influence the hunting success in your area?

Duwane Adams: I don't think it has a big influence, but it can sure hinder you if a snowstorm blows in and kills you for two or three days. Weather is usually not the big problem. Knowing where the big bucks live and how to find them is the big problem.

Carlos Gonzalez Hermosillo: It really doesn't influence us much. Hunter success is mostly influenced by the amount of game. The last snowfall was about five years ago, and it was

The intimidating cholla cactus is a favorite food for deer of the high desert. (Photo courtesy of Duwane Adams)

about an inch. We don't have much rain. If it does rain in the mountains, I'm happier than anybody else. If we get a cold front moving in the end of December or the beginning of January, the only big influence is that it starts the rut immediately. But in our operation, the weather has very little influence on our success in taking Sonoran Coues deer.

Kirk Kelso: Weather is highly significant in hunting Coues whitetails. If you have weather like rain, wind, snow, and so on, it's almost more productive to sit in camp and play cards. The Coues whitetail is a desert animal, a fair-weather animal that loves blue skies, no wind, warm temperatures, and so on. When wind and rain hit, it buries itself in a thicket and it becomes a very tough game.

How much does weather/time of season influence where and how you hunt in your area?

Duwane Adams: It doesn't affect that at all. You've got to realize that most of these deer live with less than six inches of rain a year. So when a rainstorm comes in, it's not a big deal.

Carlos Gonzalez Hermosillo: Weather has no influence at all on where and how we hunt. We just keep on doing what we know will bring success.

Kirk Kelso: The time of the season is really more important than the weather because if it's windy, rainy, or just lousy out, it doesn't matter where you hunt—you're not going to find Coues whitetails. But time of season is important. If you happen to draw a tag in Arizona and hunt during October, you've got to focus on early morning and you've got to glass into those north slopes where the deer can find shade. There's a lot you have to do when it's hot in order to find any quantity of animals. In December and January when it's cool, they're liable to be anywhere. If it's hot, you can usually still find deer, but not if it's windy and rainy.

Chapter 12
PARTING SHOTS BY THE WHITETAIL GUIDES

Do you have any unusual hunting stories to share?

Hal Blood: We had an unusual thing happen this past fall on the very last day of the season. My hunter had missed a big buck in the place we were hunting just the day before, and it had been with a doe, and we'd gone back to see if maybe they were still hanging there. We had split up, even though he didn't know the woods, and I stayed up high and let him walk down a little lower on the ridge in case I bumped something off. He must have gotten turned around and went lower than he should have, and I lost him.

We had radios, so here I was trying to figure out where he was, and it turned out he was going one way and I was going the other, and I couldn't find him. Finally he described something so that I knew exactly where he was, so I told him to stay right there and I'd come to him. I hadn't gone thirty yards when I heard "Pow, pow!" He was just sitting there when an eight-point buck walked out twenty-five yards in front of him, poking along with its head down. He shot it on the last day of the season.

Jeff Charles: We have a lot of hunters who will shoot and then quickly give up on looking for the deer. I had a man once who was on stand, and he shot at a deer. He came back to me at the truck and told me he'd missed the deer. I told him we were going to go in and take a look. He asked, "Why? I missed!" I knew from our practice session the Sunday before that this guy was a good shot, so I wanted to be sure, of course. We went in, and the area was all trampled up, but I found a place where a jay had swooped down and picked up a little bit of fat. I told the guy he had hit the deer. He was using a .25-06, a fast-moving bullet, so we didn't have much blood.

He kept saying we should quit the trail, because we weren't going to find the deer, since we were only finding a spot of blood here and there. I told him that as long as we had any blood and any daylight, we would keep going. Well, two and a half hours later we found a 225-pound eight-pointer dead with his chin right up on a log. I've found other dead deer in the woods, shot by hunters. I believe that when we make the decision to pull the trigger, we owe it to the deer to do everything we can to retrieve him.

Dan Rosman: I was out testing a grunt tube once, and about a hundred and fifty yards away was this buck, not a very big one. I hit the grunt tube once, and he grunted back right away. He came the whole distance to me down a big ravine, coming right up to me. As he got closer, his body just looked different, and I started thinking to myself, "There's something strange with this deer." I was nestled into the bottom of two pretty good-size trees, and he got to within about thirty yards, and his ears were laid back. I jumped out and clapped my hands and waved them, and that thing just kept coming!

I thought, "Dang, this thing's going to try to get me." I got back in among the trees, and when he got within about ten feet he finally recognized me for what I was, and he just bolted. It was the strangest thing, and that was the one time when I felt I was actually going to get gored by a deer. You hear about people getting hit, like the guys down in south Texas who were killed when they were rattling. That was the strangest thing that ever happened to me in hunting.

Chris Pevey: This one relates to knowing what your rifle will do. My hunter and I were in a ground blind on a food plot during the rut, and we'd seen a dandy buck in the 150 class. We spotted him, and he was working a straight line ahead of us. We didn't know the exact distance, and the guy wasn't sure what the rifle would do at longer distances. He was using a .25-06 in a Ruger One, and we'd checked the rifle the day before to make sure it was on. I was pretty impressed with the gun, and I was sure he could make the shot. I

A bow kill taken in Illinois with guide James Woodley. (Photo courtesy of James Woodley)

misjudged that buck's distance, which I thought was about three hundred yards. I told him to lay the cross hairs on his backbone, and it should drop right in. Well, he shot, and that buck looked up, and it all started going downhill after that. The buck ran directly toward us, and the hunter couldn't get another shot, because the rifle is a single shot, and he was trying to jam the second shell in backwards! That buck ran off completely unhurt.

Charles Ruth: We had a client who had hunted with us numerous times, a fellow who was an extremely good and successful hunter. One morning during the peak of the rut, we had him out on a stand way out in the sticks, far away from any farming or livestock activity. A doe came running by him panting and with her tongue hanging out, bleating like crazy. He said to himself, "What in the world? The big one must be coming!" He waited, and to his surprise, a big billy goat came trailing behind her, his coat matted up with beggar lice, chasing that doe! It caught the hunter completely off guard, and he just watched as the goat ran on after the doe. Right away, the doe ran back by him, still bleating, and right behind her was the goat again!

The hunter was really beside himself, wondering what was going on and what to do. He knew there was obviously something wrong here. The third time they came by, he ground-checked the goat with a shot from his 7mm magnum! The kicker to the story is that he had the goat caped out for a mount. We still have no idea where that goat came from, but it was sure intent on that doe!

Jay Steen: I don't have a lot of hunting-type stories, but I do remember some of the people who come in. We had a bow hunter come in who had never been here before, a fellow with long, red hair, kind of a rough-looking character. We've got some old rifles and shotguns on the walls of the rooms where the hunters stay. Everybody was eating lunch when this guy came walking in with one of those old guns. He asked me, dead serious, "Would you mind putting this thing somewhere while I'm here, because I'm on probation for a major offense, and I can't be around firearms. That's why I'm bowhunting." He came in the next day and said, "I've sure learned a lot today. That rope you gave me to get my bow back on the ground really is a neat trick. All these years I've just been throwing it down to the ground." This kind of thing kept up all week, I'm telling you. Then at the end of the hunt, this guy cleaned up, took off his wig, and introduced himself as a federal judge! He had us and all the clients completely fooled! Most of our clients are really conservative types, and he really fooled them.

David Davis: An old friend of mine shot the very best deer we ever killed. He's a guy who had hunted with me for several years on four or five different ranches. It was the last morning of the hunt, and we had some areas that I could get into and look at, then get out without disturbing anything. We had moved into three or four of these places, and we were moving on foot into the last of these places for a look-see. It was actually a wheat field, and there was a power line right-of-way going to the wheat field. We were walking along perpendicular to the power line, like you always do, and we eased up slowly, looking both ways so we could see any oncoming animal traffic. I looked to my right, and saw nothing. I looked back left, and here came a hot doe with a buck right on her, about a hundred and fifty yards away, and he was ten yards behind her in hot pursuit.

It was 35 degrees F, and there was frost all over. Every time the deer's feet hit the ground, steam was coming out their noses; it was the prettiest thing you'll ever see. They were coming almost straight toward us and would pass within a few feet of us shortly. My friend was on my right, and he couldn't see the deer. I motioned him down under a bush, one he could see under, and I stepped back enough so he could see them. I kept saying, "James, shoot the deer!" He was on his scope looking, but all he could find was the doe. I kept on whispering, "James, shoot the deer!" The doe had now come to a full stop, and I was sure the jig was about to be up! I told James firmly again to shoot the deer, and he was confused, thinking I wanted him to kill the doe. He still hadn't seen the buck.

Finally, the buck walked up beside the doe, and though he could see only the body, he could tell it was a buck, and he immediately knew I wanted him to shoot it. He shot it right in the chest with a .338. Steam came out of that deer's nose for fifteen feet when he shot, and it went right down. I said to James, "Put another shell in." He asked, "What for? The deer went down." I told him, "James, you know the rules, put another shell in, and if he even moves an ear shoot him again."

The author's Alberta buck.

He said, "What kind of deer is it?" I said, "James, what time is it?" It was 8:30, and his hunt was basically over at 11:00 A.M. I asked him, "What difference does it make? The hunt's over and it's just a buck." We watched the deer for five minutes, and it didn't move a muscle. We finally moved over toward it, and we could see one of the main beams sticking up out of the grass. As we got closer, James started moving faster, and I pulled him back and told him to slow down and be ready, in case the deer got up and tried to run. As we got closer and could see the size of the thing, James turned to me and said, "If you want to go slow, go ahead, but I'm out of here!" He ran up and slid to a stop by the deer, and was he ever a happy hunter! It was a typical ten-pointer with two extra points that scored 194. Not a bad last day's hunt!

Mike Gardner: We killed a deer this year on the last day of the season, on an evening hunt, in the last five minutes of legal shooting time, that was a 158-inch deer. We'd hunted that deer with a succession of hunters, and finally got him at the very last minute, literally.

Don White: There was one deal that really amazed me and taught me never to underestimate a deer. I had this 160-class deer all patterned; I put up my tripods, and it looked like a piece of cake. I had set up a double tripod, and I was hunting with this guy, full of confidence that the deer was going to walk out at fifty to seventy-five yards. Well, he walked out right on schedule but he was about eight hundred yards away! He stood in the middle of a *sendero* and stared at us, and I thought, "Well, there goes Plan A." That evening, when he crossed back, going from a bedding area to a feeding area, he walked out at the same place and stared at us again from eight hundred yards away. I thought, "Well, that's different; he's never done that before." I packed up the tripods, then moved seven hundred yards closer and set them back up, and thought, "We'll get him tomorrow."

Well, the next day, he walked out right on schedule, back about fifty yards from where we had first set up! I decided to stick with Plan B, and, sure enough, that night he crossed again back about fifty to seventy-five yards from the first setup. The next day, I put the tripods back in the original spot, and he crossed again eight hundred yards away! This happened four days in a row. Wherever I set up the tripods, he'd cross about eight hundred yards away. On the fifth and last day, we'd been on this deer all week, so I decided to change tactics. I put myself in the tripod, and I put the hunter in a ground blind near where the deer should be crossing. Sure enough, the next morning the deer walked out and stared at me from eight hundred yards away in the tripod. The hunter shot him in the neck at about thirty yards! He scored 166. That taught me that deer have a pattern, but also that deer can pattern you, too.

Eric Albus: I had a client from Louisiana a few years ago on a five-day bow hunt. The first night out he saw a huge ten-pointer that he was sure he was going to get the next night. We went in the next day and cut every branch from the tree he was using except one. When the deer came out that evening, it came right up to him, and when he drew his bow, one of the cam wheels squeaked, and that deer turned and walked dead away using that branch for cover all the way, never offering a shot.

The next night the hunter went back in, thinking this would be the night he'd get him. He got on the stand, and he hadn't been there long when here comes a guy in a cowboy hat, leading a horse. He led the horse up to about forty yards from his stand, took out a .44 Magnum pistol, and dispatched the horse! The guy was sitting there kind of spooked because he didn't know if somebody had shot a horse they shouldn't have shot, or what, so he just sat there until we picked him up at dark. He said, "You aren't going to believe this . . ."

It turned out that the rancher's daughter had a sick horse, and she had gone to town and got a local cowboy to put it down for her. He picked the wrong spot to do it, though. Anyway, the hunter figured the spot was ruined, but I told him to get right back in the stand forty yards from a dead horse. He probably wouldn't have done it, but he'd hunted

Coues deer country stretching to the horizon. (Photo courtesy of Duwane Adams)

with us before and had learned to trust our judgment. He went right back to the same spot, and he killed a Pope and Young ten-pointer that very night!

Keaton Kelso: I've always wanted to write a book on dumb-client stories. I had a bowhunting client one year whom we could never get into the stand until after daylight. I think he was scared of the dark. This guy was a really great shot with his bow, but everything else he did was textbook wrong when it came to hunting technique. We had target decoys out to draw in the bucks, and he was shooting his target decoys and getting down to retrieve his arrows, and he would do that all morning long.

I set him over a scrape line one time, and there was a nice licking branch hanging over the scrape. That licking branch was in his firing line, so he got down and cut it off! The list goes on and on, a textbook case of what not to do on a deer hunt. I told him to stay in his stand, and when I went to pick him up he was half a mile down in the creek bottom looking around, and he had just walked through all my bedding areas. In the end, he was upset because he didn't shoot a trophy buck.

It's one of those deals where you ask yourself, what do you do as an outfitter? He was one of those clients who called me prior to the hunt and said he was a big hunter and he had all these big trophies. I'd have to imagine that this guy had never shot a deer in his life, unless it was a little doe or a mighty unlucky buck.

James Woodley: A guy who had been out with us ten times and hadn't harvested a deer thought he wasn't going to get to come last season. He came down with cancer, and everything was on the line there for a while. They finally got all the cancer out, and he decided he could try hunting again. You talk about a guy who was just happy to be out, he was it. What happened is classic: He finally got one with his bow that scored 160, after all that effort and the considerable uncertainty caused by his health. Then some of his buddies wanted to come during gun season, so they came back with muzzleloaders and he harvested a buck that scored 185! So he went all that time without a deer, dealt with a bout of cancer, and then got two monsters in one year. A story like that can sure make you look at the things in life that are really important, and I think he came to realize that, because he just relaxed and had a good time. And it sure turned out great for him!

Gary Drinkall: Probably my best story concerns my dad. He's guided and hunted all his life, but he'd never killed a really outstanding whitetail. About three years ago we had all these does out in front of our place, and we were out hunting our butts off every day. Dad wasn't even hunting, he was out feeding cows and so forth, and while we were hunting he went for a little drive. When the rest of us got in, he told us about seeing a huge buck while he was driving around, but he hadn't been able to get a shot at it.

We thought he was blowing smoke, and we didn't really believe him, but we did keep an eye on that area, and a few days later I spotted that buck, with a pile of antlers up top, out in the field with a doe. I ran back home and told Dad the buck was there, and that if he wanted to shoot him he'd better get moving. He said he had to stay there and feed the cows, so I told him, "OK, I'm going to go shoot that buck, then." He said, "Whoa, maybe I'll go take a look." The bottom line is that he killed that deer, a massive nontypical with a gross score of 218¾! As a typical it netted 186, truly the buck of a lifetime. After fifty years of hunting, Dad finally got himself a real deer!

Rene Semple: We had a young fellow up here on a hunt-of-a-lifetime type of deal, and he'd had four open-heart surgical procedures, and he was only fifteen years old. He had really bad circulation in his heart, and he actually needed a heart transplant. His father couldn't afford the hunt, so we donated it so that they could come. His sister came along, too, and they hunted very hard for the whole time. We were down to the very last day of his hunt, and with only about three hours of daylight left this kid got a heavy old buck.

Some of our hunters were still out hunting on the last day of their own hunt, but when they heard on the radio that this kid had gotten his buck, they *all* wanted to come in! They couldn't have cared less that they were missing the last three hours of their hunt; they wanted to come in and celebrate with this young fellow. Nobody knew whether it would be this kid's last hunt or not, and they were not going to miss congratulating him. It turned out to be quite a festival. It was unusual in that I've never had a guy quit hunting in order to go and see someone else's deer, unless it was a father or someone really close to them.

Jim Shockey: I don't know how unusual it is, but I offer this as proof of the value of two things: determination, and application of sufficient time. If a hunter has sufficient time to spend on a whitetail hunt, he will be able to overcome almost any problem. I saw one buck on the second day of the season and took him seventeen days later. Another time I saw a buck on the tenth day of the season and turned him down because he was a little bit too far away. I hunted ten more days before I saw him again, this time close enough, and I got him on that shot. Another thing is that a lot of my clients will come in and say that once someone else has hunted on a stand, they don't want to hunt there anymore. On one stand during one season, exactly one week apart, we took a 148, a 166, and a 184, all from within a foot of the same spot in front of the stand.

Duwane Adams: I glassed a B&C buck one evening with a client, and we watched to see what canyon he went into. I told the client that we were going to leave at three o'clock the next morning, and it would take us at least three hours to get to that place. I told him we were going to be sitting on

An awesome lineup of bucks taken in a day of hunting in Michigan. (Photo courtesy of Bill Honza)

that rim above him, and when he comes out, we'll find him and we'll kill him. So, we were on our way up there, and we were halfway there. He told me he had to take care of bodily functions, so he went off behind a rock in the dark, and when he came back he said, "OK, let's go." Well, we took off, and we got up there and were starting to glass. I didn't glass five minutes before I found that deer, something like a 120 monster, a gigantic Coues deer.

I said, "Get your rifle ready, there's the deer!" He asked me, "Where's my rifle?" And I answered, "How would I know? You're carrying the rifle." He said, "Duwane, I don't know where my gun is." I said, "It's lying around here somewhere; where did you put it?" For maybe twenty minutes we kept up that nonsense. Finally he said, "Duwane, I left the rifle down there where I stopped on the way up!" He'd left the gun back where he'd done his business! That was an hour and a half back down the mountain.

We had a B&C buck pushing a doe at less than three hundred yards, but we had no choice. We turned around and left that monster, and walked back down the mountain. It's not like you just walk right up to this place, you know. At 2:30 in the afternoon we finally found his rifle. Well, by that time it was too late. We just turned around and went on back down to the truck. That's a true story.

Carlos Gonzalez Hermosillo: I had a hunter and a guide come upon a dead doe in a canyon while going after a nice buck. The doe was still warm, and they didn't know exactly what to make of it. They moved on past the doe to continue hunting, but shortly thereafter they heard something moving in the brush nearby. The guide told the hunter to put a round in the chamber because something unusual was happening.

Suddenly hell was upon them as a huge cougar came leaping toward them some fifty feet away! The hunter shot five times in rapid succession, but he missed every time as the cat jumped and ran in an arc around them. It did finally retreat into the brush, though, without getting to them. They quickly returned to the vehicle so they could radio me to come, and the guide told me that the cat had to be destroyed before it killed somebody. I had a cougar license in my pocket, and I arrived quickly and left the hunters with the vehicle while I went back to the dead doe with the guide.

At first we couldn't find anything, and there was no sign of the cat at all. We probed some of the dry washes near the doe, and out of nowhere came the agitated cry of a cougar. Then we saw it charging toward us through the *paloverde* brush about seventy-five feet away. A leopard had charged me in Botswana, so I had a flashback to that, but cougars in Mexico just don't do that . . . usually. I shot the animal in the left shoulder, bowling it over, and then finished it with a second shot. The cat measured seven feet four inches in length nose-to-tail. It obviously hadn't been told that Sonoran cougars don't charge!

Kirk Kelso: I had a man come to me at an SCI convention a few years ago, an older man who was overweight but who was a very happy-go-lucky guy with whom I developed a great rapport. He wanted to kill a Coues whitetail, but he really didn't seem to care if it was the biggest buck on the ranch. His physical abilities weren't good, so I said that I'd book the hunt for him with the understanding that we might not get the very best Coues deer. I let him know that he wouldn't be able to get around in a lot of that country and we'd have to stick pretty close to the truck.

Well, he showed up, and in the morning I took him personally because he'd become a pretty good friend. We left camp in the truck, and I took one of my Mexican guides, Ramon, with me. Well, we hadn't driven more than two hundred and fifty yards out of camp when we rounded a curve, and here was one of the best bucks I've ever seen in my life, standing in the road looking at us! I slammed on the brakes, and he went down into a little cut. There was no way he could come up out of that cut without climbing up three hundred and fifty to four hundred yards of open, grassy hillside across the draw. I knew that setup would enable us to shoot all day long at him from right there. So we leaped out and

This superb buck was shot in Saskatchewan with a muzzleloader. (Photo courtesy of Jim Shockey)

ran the older man up there about thirty yards, and of course he's all out of breath already as we're trying to get him set up with his bipod down.

About that time the buck showed up and started doing his tripping back and forth like Coues deer do, since they can't run straight up those steep slopes. Of course, the man started his barrage, shot up the cartridges in his magazine, and missed each shot! I had his ammo bag, and I started loading the cartridges into the chamber one at a time, and he was blazing away. Pretty soon, my Mexican guide started screaming, "*No más, no más!*" which means "No more!" I looked at Ramon, then at the deer, and it looked to me like we still had an opportunity because the deer was still in range. Ramon just got louder and more adamant, and pointed to the riflescope while still saying, "*No más!*" I looked at the scope, and the client still had his scope covers on!

He begged me not to tell the story when we got back to camp, but I told him he didn't have enough money in his checking account to buy me off telling that one! He's still a really good friend, and he hunts with us every year now. Every time he gets off the plane in Hermosillo, he says, "Now don't you tell that story," but he knows I'm going to, anyway!

What do you see as the most critical environmental/management/public relations issues affecting the future of hunting whitetails?

Hal Blood: Up here in Maine, it's managing for our critical winter habitat. The deer yards are getting logged off, and it's a major problem. It doesn't seem to be getting any better because they keep cutting them. They've got to have overstory for cover, the big spruce and fir, and some cedar for food. Adequate habitat is critical because up here if the deer don't have a place to winter, there aren't going to be any deer.

Jeff Charles: I think we have to respect the people who are against us. For example, when someone owns land they've posted, we need to respect that and stay off it. I know guys who go onto posted land, or try to get in the back side and push deer out, and so on. We've got a tremendous amount against us as it is, and we don't help ourselves when we don't respect the rights of those who disagree with us. They may not respect us, but we still need to respect them because it's the high road. They just tried to take away our bear hunt, but fortunately we won that one. However, there's already a group formed to try again to get it banned. In Maine, there are practically two different states—the southern part and the northern part. In the Portland area, there are a lot of people who have moved in from other states, and they're having a big influence. I'm afraid eventually it's going to curtail our right to hunt.

Dan Rosman: In Michigan, I think the most critical issue is management. The state manages for quantity, not quality, and I'd like to see some changes in that. For public relations, canned hunts are tough. There are these little places with fences where you go in there and shoot a deer, and you hear about that kind of thing all the time. There's a way to hunt ethically behind the fence, and the animal has as good a chance of eluding you as it does anywhere. But these little five-acre pens are a public relations disaster.

Chris Pevey: Hunters just don't get involved enough. Know who you're voting for and what they stand for. If you're a hunter and you're going to vote, make sure you know exactly where the candidate stands on hunting issues. Also, hunters need to get involved in a good organization that is actually doing something for hunting, not spending your money somewhere else and just saying they're doing it. Find out what they do and where their funds go so that you can be sure they're supporting what you love.

Charles Ruth: The major issues are habitat loss, urban sprawl, and uncontrolled development of land. The deer typically adapt to their environment, but management and public relations become more difficult with increasing deer-human interaction. There's also conflict between various user groups. Gun hunters don't like archers, and neither

Carlos Hermosillo with his wife in a room filled with incredible Coues deer trophies. (Photo courtesy of Carlos Hermosillo)

one likes muzzleloaders. Each user group typically may not want to respect the needs of the other user groups, so you can get some infighting that isn't healthy and weakens us all. Hunters are a minority, and the majority can certainly get into our business and change it if they want to. It won't be for the better if they do, I can assure you. One more thing is that we have far too many armchair biologists out there, and we need to have a reasonable amount of faith in the professional game managers and the university types who really know their stuff.

Jay Steen: We've got to get more youngsters involved in hunting to keep it going. Anything you can do to promote that would be great. Educating the public about the value of hunting as a management tool is very important, too, and we've got to educate nonhunters as to the consequences of not hunting deer. They need to understand that hunting makes for a healthy deer herd and one that's not destructive to habitat and property.

David Davis: In Texas, it's all private land, so management is the big thing. It's important to teach the average hunter and landowner good management principles. If the landowner and his neighbors could work together to manage for quality bucks, everybody would be better off. You go to a lot of deer leases that allow hunters to take one buck. That buck might be the best deer on the property genetically, yet not be old enough to be a true trophy yet. You've got to teach people the principles of taking out cull bucks as needed, and harvesting only older bucks that have good genes. It takes some education, but everybody is happier if you do that.

Mike Gardner: I see the biggest issues as expansion of the population of people and shrinking of habitat for the deer. There's overcrowding of many public hunting areas. Many of our clients who come here to hunt are disappointed with what they've been getting in terms of public hunting lands. It's becoming a problem.

Don White: In Texas and Mexico, 98 percent of the land is privately owned. We're losing large sections of land. Every generation the ranches are split among the kids, and with the next generation it gets split again. You repeat this a few times and pretty soon there's nothing but 60-acre tracts. The key to our success is 44,000 acres. Deer must have a lot of country to grow old and get big. That's really our problem down in south Texas and Mexico, because if adjacent landowners don't cooperate, you just can't grow big deer. So for us, the most critical issue is keeping big ranches intact.

Eric Albus: Environmentally, I don't know whether there are any problems, because whitetail populations are on the increase everywhere. The biggest thing I see is that we don't have very many young hunters coming along, and the hunting segment of the population is getting older and older. As hunters, we've got to start getting our kids and our neighbors' kids involved, and perpetuate, in every way we can, this great way of life we call hunting.

Keaton Kelso: Too many young deer are being killed every year. Until the Kansas wildlife management program gets a handle on the buck-to-doe ratio and tightens restrictions on the size of bucks that can be taken, our deer herd is going to gradually go down. We're seeing some states making changes. Northern Missouri has some restrictions on antler points, but in the southern part of the state any buck is still legal. Arkansas has made some changes that are positive. Here in Kansas, when I take our nice mature bucks to the cooler for processing, there are a hundred or more little forkhorns and six-pointers, all of them eighteen months old. It isn't nonresidents who are killing those yearling bucks; it's residents. We need to make some definite changes because it's not genetics that make great bucks; it's age! Fish and game departments across the country need to do whatever they can to protect younger bucks.

James Woodley: I'd say one of the biggest challenges is the animal rights movement, with attacks by groups like HSUS, where they're trying to stop hunting outright. In New Jersey they're trying to stop the bear hunt. If they stop one hunt, they won't quit until they've stopped all of them. The money it's taking to fight them is a real shame because it could be going to habitat restoration and a whole bunch of worthy projects. Politics is another one—making management decisions based on politics and emotion rather than facts. Management regimens should be set for a legitimate reason, not just because somebody wants it that way.

Gary Drinkall: In my part of the country, it's guide-resident relations. Some of the residents have their noses out of joint because guides are working and have secured the properties for paying hunters. That's something we've got to deal with somehow. What I do is stay out of the spotlight as much as possible. I don't go to any of the local shows. When we're guiding, it's straight to the property, straight to the tree stand, and then back to the camp. There's no driving around bragging and showing off what we've done. We don't let our hunters shoot at coyotes off the highway or anything like that. We're here to hunt a big deer, so let's do it smart and not create any waves.

Rene Semple: The thing that I see as critical is habitat. They say whitetails will live in the city, and they will, but they still need a habitat. Habitat loss and human encroachment are big issues. Whitetails need a place where they can live without any harassment by dogs or humans or anything else. We lose critical habitat all the time. There's a section near here that we used to hunt in, but a fellow bought it, high-fenced it, and put an elk ranch on it. We've actually shot B&C deer in that section, but now all the trees have been cut out of there, and there will never again be another wild white-tailed deer in that section. There used to be wild elk, moose, and whitetails in there, and it's sad to see a piece of prime habitat like that lost forever. We don't need any more golf courses, and we don't need any more wilderness condominiums either. The other thing is that the managers should manage the *deer*, not the *hunters*. The bureaucrats end up managing the hunters, and not the whitetails, and we have to fight with them all the time over some of the rules. On the public relations side, it's important to educate the public constantly and to promote hunting as a good, positive activity. When people ask me why I hunt, I ask them why they *don't*, because it's one of the most natural human activities on the planet.

Jim Shockey: I can't speak for other places, but in our area the most significant problem is a lack of understanding by the general public regarding the benefits of outfitting to the health of the deer herd and of the local economy. Human nature being what it is, there's a measure of envy from people in positions of power, like government officials, who might not make as much money as an outfitter does. These people, however, quite frequently control what an outfitter can and can't do. You end up with some laws that are passed more to spite the outfitters than to benefit the whitetail herds. If the government is responsible, it can be the best thing for conservation, working hand in hand with outfitters and accomplishing great things for whitetails. Resident hunters benefit, nonresident hunters benefit, the local economy benefits, white-tailed deer benefit, and ultimately even the people in government benefit, because everything is going so well. You can fight against each other or you can work together.

Duwane Adams: Builders are constructing a house a day. They're really encroaching on the habitat. I think that's the biggest problem in America today, the way builders are just eating up this country. A tract of land covered with houses can block your access to good Coues deer country.

Carlos Gonzalez Hermosillo: In Mexico, we don't have very much game except where conservation and hunting programs are in force. We have game when we take care of it. I'm afraid too many professional hunters just want the money; they drive $40,000 pickups, and they don't care about

A wall-hanger, brush-country buck. (Photo courtesy of Don White)

conservation. Only a few of us understand how important it is to have enough game to meet our commitments and meet hunters' expectations. I think game management should be done properly and should be increased in Mexico.

Kirk Kelso: I think it's unquestionably the animal rights movement. We fight activists all the time here in Arizona. They're hammering us right now over the mountain lion issue. Environmentally, where we hunt Coues whitetails is pretty remote, rugged country, so we don't have to worry about people building houses and doing those types of things, so far. In more urban areas those may be worries, but out here the influence of the animal rights movement is probably a much bigger concern.

Do you have any parting words of wisdom for whitetail hunters?

Hal Blood: Have patience and persistence. Don't give up. Too many people give up too easily.

Jeff Charles: The trophies will come, but in the meantime get out there and have a good time. Pay attention to what's going on around you so that you get the most out of the hunting experience. Don't get tunnel vision and just think about the big deer you're hoping to get.

Dan Rosman: Patience. And remember, the next hunt's always the best one.

Chris Pevey: Take a kid hunting. Get the youth involved. That's the future of hunting. Be wise about the choices you make in the deer woods, and be a woodsman and an ethical hunter. Be that way when you're outside the woods, too, even when you're talking with your buddies at the diner or somewhere, because you never know who's listening. Watch what you do and what you say, because it's critical that you make a good impression on people who know you're a hunter. I run across so many people who have the wrong impression of hunting because they've seen a certain type of hunter who represented us poorly. They haven't seen my kind of hunter, those who love the sport and are doing it for the right reasons.

A great bow kill, taken in Montana with guide Eric Albus. (Photo courtesy of Eric Albus)

I want my kids to enjoy what I've been able to enjoy, and if we aren't careful, we could lose it.

Charles Ruth: Hunt as often as you can; the wind is the number one variable; try to determine the food sources; remain flexible and keep an open mind; try a few gismos but do not rely on them. Always go back to the wind and food sources as your primary variables.

Jay Steen: Don't shoot at the antlers!

David Davis: Get out there during the rut and go hunting every chance you get.

Mike Gardner: Go south! That's what we tell our hunters when they call. If you're looking for a real giant, this isn't the place. But if you're looking for something at 150 or so, we've got the best place in North America to harvest it under fair chase conditions. You're not going to get snowed out or rained out here. If you come here on a four-day hunt, you're going to get to hunt, and you're going to see a lot of game. You'll see not just deer, but also quail, turkey, javelina, wild boar, coyotes, bobcats, rare snakes, and so on. You won't be bored because there's almost always some kind of game out in front of you.

Don White: Sit as still as you can for as long as you can. The longer you hunt, the luckier you get.

Eric Albus: For anyone who's serious about taking a trophy whitetail, you have to hunt where they are. If you've been dreaming your whole life about going on a guided hunt, don't put it off any longer. If you can in any way afford to go, do it, because you'll never regret it.

Keaton Kelso: Any whitetail hunter should learn his area and learn his deer. The whitetail brain is nowhere near as smart as the human brain, and a hunter ought to be able to be proficient with the things he has at his disposal. Do your homework on the guide and outfitter you're going to use. And remember that the tape measure does not make the trophy!

James Woodley: To sum everything up, practice, stay scent-free, and do what your guide says. Check references, too, and don't be afraid to call a few people and find out all you can about wherever you're considering hunting. Developing realistic expectations is the final thought—making sure hunters know what to expect in the way of success rates and the like.

Gary Drinkall: Just be patient, dress warmly, and know that it's going to happen. For you to shoot a trophy-book whitetail, you're going to have to put your time in, unless you're really lucky. If a trophy-book whitetail is what you're after, it might take a few hunts to do it, but you'll definitely get a crack at one eventually in this part of the world. You've got to be patient and willing to pass up lesser bucks, though. But I'd advise that if you see something you'd be happy having, go ahead and take it, even if it's not a trophy-book deer.

Rene Semple: Patience is the key. I guided for another fellow whose operation wasn't very smooth, and a doctor-client from Arkansas told me that if I ever opened an outfitting business, he'd come hunting with me. He came my first year in the business, and he shot a 184 B&C whitetail. I guess he thought there was nothing to it after that, but he's been back every year since, and yet nothing has surpassed that first one. In his case, patience is letting that 150 or 160 that walks out just keep on walking. He'll never kill one to surpass his first one if he doesn't do that, wait until the bitter end, and risk going home empty-handed. Success could happen with the first deer that comes by, but usually if a hunter is going to kill that gigantic buck, he's probably going to have to let a lot of fairly big deer walk by him. It all comes down to being patient.

Jim Shockey: There are three rules all hunters should remember: Deer do what they do, deer are where they are, and deer move when they move. The ultimate rule in whitetail hunting is that time is your number one tool to get a big buck.

Duwane Adams: For Coues deer hunters, the best advice is this: Get a good pair of binoculars and learn how to glass with it from a tripod. Once you learn that, the next step is to get your shooting up to par. Then concentrate on keeping your physical conditioning at a good average, and you're going to have a good chance of taking a quality buck. There are a lot of bucks out there that people never see, and if you just do these things, you've got a good chance of taking a great buck every year.

Carlos Gonzalez Hermosillo: The Coues deer is one of the most interesting trophies to take, being a great challenge because of the rough terrain, the wariness of the species, and the long distances involved. I think it's very important for the real hunter to experience this animal.

Kirk Kelso: For anyone who aspires to hunt the Coues whitetail, prepare yourself to get hooked on the sport. It is really a neat game, and these little deer will test your limits. I'll tell anybody who comes with us to be prepared to come back. It's that addictive.

SAFARI PRESS